THE

FIVE

GEMS

Jenni Lloyd

DEDICATION

To my Father God - with Him NOTHING is impossible, but without Him nothing makes sense! May all these stories be for your Glory, King Jesus!

This book is dedicated to my husband, Michael and my children Mikaela, Connor, Starla, Tayla and Levi who have made me into the woman I am today.

Michael, you have always been my one and only, my best friend, the incredible father to our beautiful children and husband who gives so much of himself to our family.

I am so incredibly grateful to live life with you, to laugh and cry, dream and grow, and to raise our children together, serving and loving Jesus always. I love you always and forever.

You, my 5 gems are incredible in every way, you are our delight and joy, and I love you with all my heart.

To my Dad and Mum, Keir and Callie Tayler who have encouraged and loved me always and have modelled what it is to love Jesus and say YES to Him above all others.

To my brother Simon and his wife Nicole (who I also get to call sister), who are my friends not just family. You have given so much to help me get this book published. For my nephews Nathan and Sean Tayler, you are strong courageous boys who have an incredible future and I love being "your favourite Aunty Jen" - Thank you!

To my sister Lisa who is also my best friend, and her husband Peter (who I also get to call brother). You have always encouraged me, been a wise sounding board and in every season have let me be real. For my nieces Amy and Katie, you are beautiful young girls who have a delightful future. I love you so much. Thank you!

To my other Dad and Mom - Dave and Pam Lloyd, who have embraced me as their own daughter when I married their son, Michael. They are unwavering in their love for Jesus and for others.

To my valued, deeply loved friends … Helen Aitchison, Caron Lloyd, Tanya Olivier, Angela Morgan, Kerry Robinson, Tamara Vercueil and Claire Wienand … you are treasures and I love you.

FOREWORD

I'll never forget the first time I met Jen. Her beautiful twins weren't even a year old, but this woman was the quintessential picture of a mother. She had only recently come through the expansion of her family from 3 to 5 children, but remained poised, calm and keen for connection. We hit it off immediately and have been close friends ever since that winter evening back in 2011. Some of my favourite moments in life are the mornings that Jen and I get together to catch-up, usually at her home or mine. The tray is set, the teapot filled, and the conversation flows as much as the tea!

She has been a huge source of encouragement and strength to me, a true ally, as we navigate our way through the challenges of parenting in a post-modern world. I can count on her for sound and sane advice and her voice is always one of faith.

Jen is as gentle as she is determined. She is a devoted, consistent and God-fearing mother who's on top of it all, without being so perfect that we cannot relate to her. She loves fiercely, gives whole-heartedly and leads uncompromisingly. Her journey as a Mom has not been without its challenges. In fact, I have watched Jen come through many storms, but, somehow, always with resilience and with much grace. She's unrelenting in her desire to raise a Godly family, tireless in her work and sets a fine example in her community.

This book is a gift to us - a large and treasured piece of Jen's heart. In it, we get to go into her home, sit around the table with her family and glimpse inside her beautiful soul.

This is Jen's unique story, her tale of life as a wife, mother, daughter, sister, friend, leader, athlete and home-maker. Read it to learn; read it for courage; read it to grow. May it nourish your inner being, inspire you for more, and cheer you on in whatever stage of the race you may be.

- Angela Morgan
  Johannesburg

My sister, Jenni Lloyd is a working mother of five children by day and a writer by night. She is the eldest of 2 siblings and "mothered" her baby brother and sister from the tender age of seven. Jenni is a woman of incredible courage, strength and depth. She values the Word of God as the core of her family and a compass though life. She is not only my older sister, but a mentor, a friend and an inspiration to me and so many others. As a little girl, she became my hero, throughout my teen years she became my role model and as an adult, she is my best friend. I watched my big sister grow up, fall in love, get married and have her first baby. It is because of her that I desired to be a wife and a mother and now I am one. Jenni started writing this book when my daughters were babies and the thoughts and revelations in her book have deeply affected and shaped my perspective on motherhood and womanhood. Jenni's words have a way of lifting your head to see the big picture, even in the craziness and mess we call life.

Her book reflects her heart as she navigates the daunting and adventurous rapids of, not only parenting but character, life, marriage and virtues.

Jenni and her husband, Michael have been married for 21 years and together they lead and serve in their local church in Bryanston, Sandton, Johannesburg.

- *Lisa Haynes, Sister*
  Redding California

Jenni, my big sister and friend, has always been a pillar of strength and a source of wisdom. Growing up, Jen was always diligent, focused and composed. As a mother, she guided my wife and I through the tricky paths of early parenthood with such an ease and encouragement. No matter how tired or distressed we were (or she was), she always brought a calm and ease to every situation.

This book documents her journey. As she's raised her incredible children in accordance to God's Word, she effortlessly writes of her journey in a typically 'Jenni' fashion – nothing is too big or too difficult for our God so long as we pause and ask God to show us the bigger picture.

- *Simon Tayler, Brother*
  Ballito, Kwa-Zulu Natal

CONTENTS

ACKNOWLEDGMENTS

Mikaela, our eldest daughter. You made me into a mother - you are my beautiful, gentle, kind and loving devoted girl who loves deeply. You are a delight. I adore you.

Connor, our son who is brave and wise, with leadership in his destiny. You make us laugh so much and I love your sense of fun. Watching you grow into a mighty man is wonderful. I love you so much.

Starla, my cuddly, sweet, gentle girl who loves with all her heart and gives her very best always. You are our special noodle-bug and I love you so very much.

Tayla, my other special girl who is full of life and spunk, adores animals, who has a laugh that is so contagious and beautiful. You are so precious, and I love you always.

Levi, my brother bear, with blonde straight hair who is courageous, strong, kind and so diligent.

What a joy you are, and I am so grateful to God for our extra surprise package of you and your twin sister.

This book is dedicated to you, My 5 gems!

My little gems fill this crown I wear

Full of diamonds that I share

It is for my King, to bring Him joy and glory

As He gave me these gifts, it is my story.

To capture special moments and them to treasure

Has great value, there is no measure

So, this is my story, my family of seven

I want to represent His name and a little bit of heaven

FROM THE AUTHOR

So here begins our story …

I hope you enjoy, for this is an expression of my heart, the primary purpose is to encourage and have fun, to share tips and hints, and life as it is done here is South Africa raising "the big 5" children - 3 girls and 2 boys.

Please don't "mark" me or judge me, but rather read, have a laugh or maybe a cry at times. I want my life to count and the input I have into these little lives that are entrusted to me, is HUGE! We all need encouragement or if nothing else just good old plain realness, vulnerability and trusted friends.

It is on-going, this learning of being a mum to these precious 5, at the University of Parenthood in the season called LIFE. But I am not alone, as I have a great family, an extended family (who don't all live too close to me sadly) and a wonderful "hands on" loving husband who adores his children, and but MOST importantly, I have the best parenting reference in the world - the Bible!

I will write what I feel in my heart - it may be deep, it may be light-hearted. Whatever it may be, I see it as an "offloading", or as an easy, fun way of documenting all things practical, funny and possibly a good idea. There may be very serious times too - times of reflection, times of recalling and times of expressing the treasures of God's word.

My daily cry or prayer to my Heavenly Father, is to help me see what you see, love like you love and to lift my vision higher! In the moments of chaos, noise, whining (my worst!) and sibling teasing, I try to breathe - DEEPLY - and look to Him for wisdom, grace and lots of patience.

So often I wonder how 5 little people can come from the same gene pool yet be so very different. It amazes me! I often watch them play and interact, and I think, oh my goodness, these children are mine and yet all are so unique. I dream for them, and wonder what they will be and do one day in the future, then I stop as I don't want them to grow up. Being a mother has brought out so many different facets in my life - things I already knew were there all along, and other things I didn't ever expect.

As I am quite a perfectionist, my standard is high - both on myself and those who are in my life. This is both a good and bad thing. I have learnt, and am still learning, that some battles are worth fighting and other are not. For example, in our home there is zero tolerance for ugliness, nastiness or fighting and hurting one another. It does happen - let's be real, BUT we "nip it in the bud" asap. I always tell my children, "do you see mom and dad fighting like this, being nasty, name calling etc." - and of course the answer is no. Children do model what that see and not what you say. You cannot fool them! I once heard a great saying that the best gift you can give your children is a happy secure marriage.

I

NO FEAR OF THE FUTURE

When we found out I was expecting twins at just 6 weeks into the pregnancy, more than anything I was terrified of how we were going to afford feeding, clothing, educating and just generally providing for our big family, as going from a family of 5 to 7 is huge and is abnormal. I remember a dear friend saying to me at that time, be encouraged as God knows what he is doing, God knows the plans, and he would not give you the toys without the batteries. That last statement may seem trivial but let me tell you how very encouraging that was to me. As a "planner" and a person who likes to be organized, this came as a massive shock as this was not "in my plan". Who was I that I had the audacity to question God, the creator of the universe, I realized how very selfish and ridiculous that was. In the quiet moments, I remember being led to read the account of Mary when she was told she would conceive supernaturally the Son of God. Can you imagine how that must have felt? Just consider it for 20 seconds ... Then her response is key, she says, "May it be unto me according to your word" - Luke

1: 38. From that moment, I chose to believe it was his will and plan for our lives.

One of my favourite books of the Bible is Proverbs. I remember as a young girl of seven years old, my father teaching me a proverb a week. It doesn't sound like much, but each Proverb has SO much wisdom that it takes me a while for my mind, heart and soul to absorb it. I must read this Proverb from the Scriptures again and again, for it to sink in. It is a promise from the Most High God who loves me. What a beautiful promise to be clothed in strength and dignity, to laugh without fear of the future!!

Strength is the power to resist attack, to be impregnable, to resist strain or stress and to be durable. It is to maintain a moral or intellectual position.

Dignity is to be of quality of being worthy of esteem or respect. An inherent nobility and worth, poise and self-respect.

Laugh is to feel a triumphant or exultant sense of well-being.

One just must look at the economics of the world we live in and fear can easily take root, yet I look not to this world but to the promises my Father in Heaven has lavished on me.

What a privilege to raise children today, to be a part of the army that is advancing and taking ground spiritually. Yes, it is hard, yes, it is expensive and yes it can be scary, BUT I choose not to dwell on that, but rather dwell on the Word, the Truth. This is of course a lesson in progress and there are times when I feel very strong and other times I feel totally overwhelmed with the costs of living. I have noticed that when my soul has not been fed with the word and I have got caught up with doing life, my fear is more evident.

You see, life is about ALL about choices. I chose to see my challenging circumstances as a blessing. And so, I will choose to be believe in faith what the Word says, "to be clothed in strength and dignity, and to laugh without fear of the future." My future is full of promise because of WHO I serve. I choose to laugh when financial fear sets in, I will not be depressed after a weekly grocery shop or moan or whine because of what I see, but I choose to trust Him and lean not on my own understanding as I choose to walk with Him and acknowledge Him in all my ways!

So, I will resist strain or stress and be durable, to have inherent nobility and worth, poise and self-respect, and to feel a triumphant or exultant sense of well-being, when I consider my future.

2

BUILDING HOUSES

How to build your house?

I love watching HOME programs on refurbishing, redecorating and all those inspiring programs. One of my favourite magazine is the home interior types as there are so many wonderful, and often such simple ideas. There is always an opportunity to try something new and shuffle furniture around for a different look etc. My kids have always been exposed to this, as change in our home design is regular – its good and fun.

This got me thinking on a deeper level ....
Proverbs 14: 1 "The wise woman builds her house, but with her own hands the foolish one tears hers down."
You know those funny sayings: "A happy wife = a happy life" or "when mama ain't happy, ain't nobody happy"! This can be true as everything tends to revolve around the woman / wife / mother of the house.

So, what is a house and what is its purpose?

In my opinion, a house is:

- a covering, a protection from the elements,
- it accommodates all one's possessions and keeps it safe.
- It has walls or boundaries, it is a place of refuge, a place of familiarity.
- It also offers identity as people know where to find you.
- It can also be a place of nourishment (food), rest and cleansing.

101   Construction :

1.   The foundation – this I believe is trust. Without trust, there is a rocky foundation, an unstable building, a dodgy wobbly home.

2.   Next, we start with the framework which is prudence – prudence sees the big picture

and then acts. It is about focuses on what counts!

3. Then there is the roof – which is wisdom Prov 8: 12 – "I, wisdom, dwells together with prudence, I possess knowledge and discretion!" How do we do life without wisdom? Wisdom is wise because she LISTENS!

How then do houses fall apart?

Well, I believe it is the little things – Songs of Solomon says in 2:15 – "catch for us the foxes, the little foxes that ruin our vineyards, our vineyards that are in bloom!"

- it's the little bits and pieces that fall through everyday life
- the belittling of one another's needs and desires
- the offences (usually small) that are overlooked
- The lack of "accommodating" one another, selfishness – this is a BIGGY!

So, in summary, I want to build a home that has a strong firm foundation of trust, a safe and secure place for my husband, my children and even one day their children. To build a structure or framework of prudence, foresight, knowledge and of vision of the bigger picture in growing this family, and constantly asking for wisdom at every step. You see, it's not about where you live or what you live in, but who you are with and influence for the higher calling.

3

GET REAL!

I had a rough week last week, one thing on top of the next caused me to lose my sense of humor in a big way! To know when a stranger looks at me (like really looks at me for more than 3 seconds) and smiles with her eyes, then says a few kind words, I start to well up with tears, that's when I know I am feeling tender. For someone who doesn't wear her heart on her sleeve, nor cry easily, this was just one of those weeks. I am certainly not proud of it, but I am also being real.

When I look at my 5 children, the ones who "squawk" the loudest get the immediate attention, but sometimes it is the quieter ones who possibly need the biggest hug or the smiling eyes! I guess for me this last week, I needed to squawk but I didn't and so the smiling eyes of some random stranger, brought big tears to my own eyes. There are moments when a good cry is wonderful. It gets all the emotions out, it "cleanses" the soul and unburdens the heart. After a very long week and a few hiccups, I had a good sob and then the world looked better – just like after a good rain!

There are times when I wonder if having a brave face and saying" it's all fine and good" is really a strength of character or is it more of a covering up? Our lives tend to leave us so busy and rushed that to take the time to ask the question – "how are you?" – one only hopes the answer is "fine" and nothing more!

Maybe we should be asking the "right" questions?! To ask a question that cannot be answered with just "fine" may be the solution. Some examples could be, "Did you sleep well last night?" or "Did you go away for the weekend?" – being a bit more creative with the question, can often lead to a more telling result.

I am going to ask some more pointed questions this week and maybe there will be a moment when I can give a hug to a random stranger or a smile, because I have taken the time to LOOK that person in the eyes and take notice! It can mean so much to someone to just be kind.

4

KEEP ON KEEPING ON

In June annually, our country hosts the famous Comrades Marathon in KwaZulu Natal. It always makes me think of all the shapes, sizes, ages, races and gender running this incredibly taxing and exhilarating race (so I am told – not totally convinced about the exhilarating side but will take their word for it!)

One of my earliest memories of athletics, was when we lived in Zimbabwe and I was in Std 2 / Grade 4 – it was our inter- house sports day. At the start of my race, I saw my Dad at the end of the lane (which seemed SO far away). As the gun fired and we started running our hearts out, I saw and heard my Dad shouting and encouraging me and jumping around. Somehow, I won that race – never to be repeated – winning athletic races that is! It was the best feeling having him so focused on me and no matter what the outcome was, he was my biggest fan regardless of where I came. I was thrilled to have finished it! I have a photo of this in my album and it always brings back such amazing memories.

When I watch the end of the Comrades marathon I am almost always in tears at the joy of the ones who have crossed over the finish line, and yet also the incredible disappointment and sense of failure for those who don't make the cut off initially, then those who fail to finish minutes, and even seconds before the gun fires that it is the end! Some run across so tired but smiling, others collapse literally at the line and others cry. I have huge admiration for these competitors – it is an amazing accomplishment but still doesn't make me EVER want to do it.

You see, this life we live is in fact a race. It's not about how fast you run, who you are, what your story is, what you wear or how perfect your technique is – it is about finishing! No matter what you have achieved, your qualification, your culture, your wealth or status – in this race we are only but runners like in Comrades and the goal is to finish!

The runners I have spoken too have said that what keeps them going are the supporters on the sidelines.

There are stages in our "race/life" where we have incredible support – people cheering us on and encouraging us to keep going – friends, family and even strangers. Then we hit quiet parts of the road, where we hear nothing but our pounding heart, our heavy breathing and the thumping of every step. We keep on as we know soon enough, we will be surrounded by the support again, but in the mean-time we dig deep and set our mind and hearts and keep on keeping on!

1 Corinthians 9:24-25 (NIV)
24 Do you not know that in a race all the runners run, but only one gets the prize? Run in such a way as to get the prize. 25 Everyone who competes in the games goes into strict training. They do it to get a crown that will not last, but we do it to get a crown that will last forever.

3D VISION

Most movies now seem to have the 3D option for viewing, where it all seems so real, so alive! But we get to wear these very nerdy, uncomfortable glasses in order to fully appreciate the 3D.

I don't know about you, but my eyes take a bit of time adjusting to the glasses and then to the movie. Imagine not being able to see in 3D? To only see 'flat' 2D pictures. There is no substance, no depth, no shape – how very boring and limiting. Sometimes, we need to look beyond our own comforts, our own perspectives and to see the things or the purpose of our life from a new dimension.

Our perspective and interpretation of how we see our life is limited by our vision!

Seeing clearly is a gift! I am not just talking about the literal vision of good sight, but also to be enabled to have clear direction, vision or purpose for life. Sight is seeing what is in front of me, vision is looking beyond that, to seek or search, a quest for something, a journey of discovery.

We have this funny saying in our family – "Looking like a Lloyd" – it is a phrase that has stuck! Often the kids will say they can't find something, and they have looked everywhere. Knowing that this is probably not 100% true, I usually respond by saying, "Are you looking like a Lloyd?" – meaning, have your really searched or have you just "scanned" for the item?

There are times when things are so obvious, and other times when it takes some effort, some searching. It usually takes more than just a quick scan, it takes effort, time and patience, but once it is found – what joy!
Don't just take life at 2D, search for the deeper dimension – see life in 3D!

What we see is mainly what we look for ....
But _seek_ first the kingdom of God and his righteousness, and all these things will be added to you – Matt 6: 33

6

THE SMALL SPARKS START THE BIG FIRES

We recently had a very cold evening and are lucky enough to have a fireplace in our home – not the instant gas ones, but the good old-fashioned log fire. As we sat chatting, we soon fell silent and were mesmerized by the crackles of wood burning, the intense orange, yellow and red flames and the hiss of the heat. I don't know what it is about fires, but to watch a log fire to me is one of the most relaxing things, a simple pleasure!

This got me thinking about an African proverb I heard recently – *"the little sparks start the big fires."* How true and how profound. So often it is the little things, the little signs of life or encouragement or it can be the little niggles, the little ignition resulting in a huge fire, a roaring destructive furnace. All it takes is one spark!

I know that I fall prey to this so often especially in moments of frustration or tiredness, where my tongue is quick, and it can spark something, it can set ablaze a whole forest! How sobering ... in us all we need to watch, listen and pay attention to the small areas of our lives – how we speak to our children when no one is watching, how we honour our spouses in public and private, how we treat our employees etc. All this counts, as all of this affects someone as soon as it leaves our mouth.

My desire is to spark into flames great passion for life, and for the one who gave it to me. I want to spark in my children a desire to pursue valuable things in life, to notice the small things while dreaming for the biggies!

It reminds me of James 3: 5
"So also, the tongue is a small member, yet it boasts of great things. How a forest is set ablaze by such a small fire!"

7

WIDE OPEN SPACES

Open places, no fences, no walls
Big green spaces, freedom to fall
Laughing, dancing, twirling and running
Giggles, fresh air and sunning
African plains, hot desert sun
Horizons, sunsets, storms that come
Fever trees, grasslands, open spaces
Wide, 'boundary-less', open places

There is nothing more spectacular than seeing a gorgeous sunset or sunrise over the African plains, or the majestic mountains and their incredible vastness. I think in each of us there is this desire to see space, to see open-ness as far as the eye can see – wide open spaces. It resonates within us the freedom, the open-ness, the liberating of self in these physical spaces.

I think we must intentionally create pockets of open spaces – to make space for space! Our lives are so constricted and restricted to structure and boundaries, which is of course good, but like everything there must be a balance, there must be some moderation. I love structure, I love boundaries and I think they are so important especially in raising children, as well as in life generally. With boundaries comes security, but also there is a time and a place for "boundary-less" spaces (if there is such a word).

I am a disciplined person, but with having 5 children, I can't always have "my ducks in a row", and that is also ok. Jesus has come to give me life and to live more abundantly, so if I constantly "box" Him in and not allow His freedom, am I in fact living an abundant life, a free life with Him?

Freedom sets us apart from the bondage of life. The weight of life can wear us down, it can hinder us from what we are called to do. Note to self – Live in this FREEDOM – the wide-open spaces, breathing slowly and deliberately, taking one day at a time but seeking wisdom all along the way.

8

PERFECTLY ORDINARY DAYS

There are days where life seems very ordinary, very boring almost. I think what can sometimes wear us mothers down is that life can be very monotonous – it's the same routine every day, regardless of weekends or weekdays. Yet how one sees ordinary is very subjective. The definition of ordinary is "with no special or distinctive features or of no exceptional ability, degree, or quality" – it's average or normal.

How I may deem or see ordinary is perhaps in your eyes exceptional, or even below average. Whichever way one looks at it, the monotony of being a mother can also be perfectly ordinary in our eyes, but in our children's eyes it can be an extra special day. The faithfulness of the small stuff equates to big stuff one day, and before you know it, your once completely dependent baby is now feeding itself, then walking, then dressing, then going to school, then leaving home.

I have struggled many a time (and sometimes still do) with those perfectly ordinary days, as I like to "achieve", to get out, to do etc. I have lists to work through and feel a sense of achievement when they are done – ok, I know that sounds funny, but that is who I am – true story! Having littlies changes all of that and the seasons of being at home doing play dough, puzzles, swinging, reading the same story night after night, making food or meals constantly can be so frustrating, yet so incredibly rewarding and humbling. In their eyes (our children) we are their heroes! We provide, entertain, nurture, cuddle, feed, play, bath and read all in one day, and then do it again the next day and the next! Yes, it is ordinary in our eyes and can seem so boring, BUT in their little eyes, we are exceptional, special and are their heroes.

To all of you and to me – don't despise the perfectly ordinary days, because each day is a gift, it is a moment to treasure. Time does not stand still, and we don't want to wish our lives away or live for the next big moment.

Psalm 119: 105 (The Message) says, "Your word is a lamp unto our feet". It is not a spotlight or a head-lamp, it is a lamp which lights our way, one step at a time. Take one moment at a time, one day at a time, as it is ok to have a perfectly ordinary day!

9

SIMPLE PLEASURES

Sometimes it is the simple pleasures that make us smile, laugh and have the most fun. I know with my children the most wonderful entertainment is water – pouring it, splashing in it, making mud pies, making rivers and waterfalls, and then also bubbles. To play and see the joy on their faces in these moments is priceless!

When life gets too busy, too complicated and too stressful, take a moment to sit and write a list of simple pleasures. Recently in the holidays, my children uttered these terrible words – "I'M BORED! I have NOTHING to do!" – well that makes me see red instantly. So, after a deep breath, I sat them down and told the older ones to write out a list of ALL the many things they can do with what they have at home, which doesn't cost money. After a few brief minutes, the list was a page long! Next, we stuck these on their cupboard doors and agreed that every time they said they were BORED, they had to choose one of these things to do. Some of the examples were: baking, shooting hoops outside, building a fort, reading, climbing trees and making a rally track for cars (boy option), writing or drawing about a topic I gave them each day (this was fun and yet a big learning curve too for them) ... back to the simple, normal things using a wonderful underestimated tool in today's world – *IMAGINATION*!

This soon became fun and the selecting from the list was in fact interesting and it's kind of empowered them to be the leader in their own world and make their day fun and exciting. It was not always up to MOM to find ways to entertain them, but they had to do it and not use electronics in this – challenging I know, BUT it is possible!!

Even as adults, we sometimes forget or nullify the simple pleasures! Maybe writing a list of these would be a great reminder of what we do have and what we can do outside of being entertained in the "lazy" way.

I can pretty much guarantee that most of the time it *doesn't cost anything but has great value*!

ASSET MANAGER

During a school concert not so long ago, I was seated next to another mother (a familiar face but not someone I know), so of course we got chatting about which class our kids are in and the "small chat" of school life etc. Then the question was asked, "so how many kids do you have?" – I have come to love this question, as the responses I get are priceless – I could even write a whole book on what gets said to a mom of 5! She of course, gasped in shock and then we chatted a bit more. Sometime later, she turned to me and said something that has stuck with me – a profound statement … "You are so *rich and so wealthy*. You know, no one will ever ask how much you have in your bank account, but they will always ask how many children you have!"

That statement has really stood out for me as it has made me count the blessings over, and over again. It is abnormal, it does shock most people and they can say the most bizarre things, yet it has opened so many doors of conversation – a testimony of God's goodness and blessing and provision! I have random people pouring out their hearts to me sitting on the beach, at a play-ground, at a hospital, waiting in a queue or in a lift etc. and it never ceases to amaze me how God uses this every time. Maybe one feels 'safe' talking to a mum of five kids – there is a vulnerability, honesty, identity, a safe place – I'm not sure? But what I do know is that my Father uses every situation for HIS GLORY, and if this is my small part, then thank you Jesus as without you it is impossible and abnormal, but in His will it is a joy, delight and great blessing.

As I have worked in the financial world and have some formal education in this, when I am asked at a party or social function what I do, I now don't just say I am a mum. I say I am an asset project manager! Sounds important and clever hey? But more than that it is true! I organize, run and oversee the most unique, special, valuable, high fund assets that are going to yield massive returns for HIS GLORY! Of course, I choose who I say this too, but I am so tired of being dismissed for just saying I am a mum. This job is the most wonderful and yet hardest job ever.

Don't just call me "MUM" – call me an asset manager!

II

HIDDEN HUNGER

I learnt something new this week about a term
called "hidden hunger. "This is used to describe
children who appear on the surface to look healthy
enough but internally their bodies are starved or
stunted of essential vitamins and minerals for
optimum growth and potential. In my country this
is a huge problem! Mostly the hidden hunger
refers to children who get enough calories for
them to function in day-to-day activities, but their
bodies are physically and mentally stunted. These
same children tend to eat mainly from only one
food source i.e. loads of carbs and sugars. Globally
stunted growth and anemia in children are a major
cause of health problems in later years, particularly
the increasing prevalence of overweight/obesity
and chronic diseases such as diabetes, blood
pressure issue etc. This has terrible personal and
social consequences. It also results in a double
burden for the health systems, with massive health

costs and a negative impact on economic productivity. The impact of hidden hunger is huge!

This can relate to our well being too – we appear to "have it all together" on the surface of life, yet we are starved and stunted emotionally, mentally and spiritually. We overindulge from the wrong sources and although this may sustain us, we are at risk of developing long lasting problems. I can relate this to so many areas in my life, but in this case, I want to talk about parenting. Of course, I want to feed my children well in a literal sense, but more than that I want their souls to be well nourished so that they can   reach the full potential God has for them, and to grow and mature as strong whole individuals who don't have emotional baggage and stunted levels of maturity. I want them to go further and do better than we do, and for their children to excel even more. We can't do this on our own, but we can ask for wisdom, and our Heavenly Father will not withhold it.

There are so many sources from which to glean knowledge and understanding regarding parenting. Sometimes an over bombardment of information causes an imbalance in what we draw from and how we apply it to our own lives.

Although knowledge is power (so they say), I believe wisdom is life!

12

ADVENTURE JUNKIES

The other day I was sitting in a coffee shop and overheard a conversation of two men talking about their recent adventure mountain bike race etc. The conversation went on and on about the gear they buy (the cost is frightening let me tell you!) and their "war wounds" etc. – you know how men are with their battle scars?! I then went into my own "pondering state" and wondered why there is such a huge following of men and women doing adventure races, endurance races whether on bicycle or foot, climbing mountains both near and far, doing the whale to wine routes – you know, the list is endless. Twenty years or more ago, these kinds of things were not so dominant and addictive.

Why?

I guess it is because our lives are incomplete on so many levels ... we work too hard, spend too much time in the offices, cars, meetings and so on. There has become a dissatisfaction, an unfulfillment of life and more and more people are searching for a satisfaction. Sometimes I think these things can become idols in our lives where it is an all-consuming hobby or quest or discovery. It "eats" into our family times and our weekends. I don't think these things are wrong but there is a balance that is needed. To prioritize I believe in setting these in place – God first, family second, ministry third, work and others next.

In life there is always balance needed. How we achieve this is all very personal and we need to ask God for wisdom. In the Bible, Solomon who was a great King, was told by God that he could ask for anything. Imagine that?! So, the thing he asked for was wisdom! He became the wisest, and wealthiest man ever. I wonder if that same question was asked of us today, what would our response be? I am sure most people would want wealth or time? But wisdom is key in how we live our lives, the examples we set for our peers and our children who watch us very closely. Achieving balance in our lives today, requires great wisdom but all we need to do is ASK!

Adventure junkie or not, I guess we so often need a rush of adrenalin (well some more than others, let's be honest!), or something to work towards. I hope that I set an example to my children of always having my priorities right, and to keep the main thing, the main thing!

13

MEMORY BANKS

I heard this mentioned the other day and it got me thinking of all the happy memories I have and how rich my memory bank is. What a privilege to have a memory bank that has a big fat balance of good, joyful memories as a child, a teenager and as an adult. I thought I would share some …

Some of my great memories are of me riding a motorbike with my dad – I must have been about 3 and sat in front of him while the wind whipped through my hair and I felt so safe and happy. Another is of me learning my timetables day in and day out, but the reward was so worth it as I got my longed-for Peach Blossom "my little pony".

Then there are holidays where we had the most amazing memories as children – crab hunting at night on the beach with torches, making log fires in the mountains, roasting marshmallows and learning to ride horses. I know it sounds so idyllic and it was – how incredibly blessed I feel that I have such awesome memories. I am sure I have some not so pleasant memories but somehow, I can't recall them as the happier ones carry far more "weight" in my memory bank!

The other big ones are finishing school, going overseas, getting engaged to the love of my life and best friend, walking down the aisle with my Dad and then my Dad doing the wedding ceremony, playing the song "Butterfly Kisses" to my Dad at our reception – whenever we hear this song, both my mum and dad and I start to cry as it holds such a special place in our hearts.

Then it was the finishing my degree, travelling with my hubby to some of the places we wanted to go to for years before, then the birth of all my children (each one has its own set of memories and stories), teaching them to ride a bicycle … the list is endless and each day another memory gets added.

I would hate to lose my memory - to not have any reference points, or milestones to reflect on or stories to tell. Another thing to be grateful for – to remember and recall special and happy events.

The great thing with my memory bank is that there is no limit to the transactions, deposits and there are often withdrawals (the re-telling of stories) but the balance only increases, day by day.

I want to help fill the memory banks of my children with such special times/ deposits. It doesn't have to be an overseas trip, or anything elaborate (although those are dreams and one day will happen!), it can be each day. It can be teaching them to fry an egg, tie their shoe laces or playing UNO in front of the fire one cold winter's night.

Every day is a gift – make it count and bank those memories!

14

HANDS

One thing I often notice about people are their hands – it is not necessarily the most manicured perfect hands that get my attention, but rather the ones with "character" i.e. hands that have a few scars, "well used hands", sometimes even nail bitters ... it makes me wonder why they bite nails, or why the hands are so "worn". I loved my Granny's hands. They were soft and beautiful – not because they were perfect and unblemished, but rather because of what they did and how they loved me. She baked, loved, cooked, cleaned, wiped, knitted, wrote, drove, gardened, helped and nurtured. Her hands represented the life she lived – one of a hardworking woman, a woman who gave unselfishly and loved unconditionally.

I also love the hands of babies – tiny, tight fists that often have fluff between their fingers, toddlers' hands who have soft dimples in the place of knuckles, and children's hands who are learning to hold crayons to draw and discover creating. Hands tell so many stories. I always tell my children after any outing or before eating food – "have you washed your hands?" So often after school, their hands tell their own story – a combination of sand, dirt under fingernails, sticky glue, or coloured paint or even a scratch or two. It is a good indication of how school went that morning – a fun, happy day doing life as you do as either a 3-year-old or 12-year-old!

Our hands have such a vital role to play in how we love one another, how we give, how we work, how we worship and even how we fight. Hands have so much to offer – they touch, show affection and love, defend, discipline, worship, pray, seal a deal (handshake), to meet and greet, give, heal, help, create … you get the picture? The Bible talks of Jesus sitting at the right hand of God – He is God's Son and "right-hand man" – a man of importance and significance. This summarizes who Jesus is to me – He is my healer, He is who I worship, He is my deliverer and protector.

I want to use my hands more for loving than defending or fighting. I want to have clean hands and a pure heart, hands that one day, when I am old, I will not look at and think they are ancient and worn, but rather hands that have loved and given SO much – hands that tell stories and display His glory in all I do.

Psalms 24: 4 He who has clean hands and a pure heart.

15

GREAT & NOBLE

*"I long to accomplish a great and noble task, but it is my chief duty to accomplish small tasks as if they were great and noble." — **Helen Keller**

I saw this quote the other day and it REALLY got to me. It is incredibly profound! It can be related to any aspect of life, across any nationality, culture, status, gender or age.

I totally "get" this as I sometimes wish I was achieving something great and noble. But who determines what is great and noble?

- Is it traveling the world?
- Is it mentoring?
- Is it achieving several degrees?
- or being the CEO of a large corporate?

What is it exactly that is great and noble?

If you give it some thought, what would you come up with? I bet it is all subjective, and no matter what YOU think is great and noble, is often seen completely differently by someone else.

You see, it doesn't matter what the task is but rather what my attitude is like in achieving this task. So, for me the, the small tasks are mundane and at this stage seemingly insignificant to me, but one day they will count. For now, my primary task at hand is being a mother. I am in the training stage – manners, chores, attitudes correction etc. etc. It is a job that requires doing the small tasks repeatedly, most often with no different results such as repeating the phrase, "Say thank you!" Eat with your mouth closed." Soon this will come naturally to them (well let's hope) and then an ungrateful, selfish little person who is adorable and cute incredibly emerges into a polite child who then matures and becomes a well-mannered, respected adult.

That is something that will always be admired, just like the saying, "Manners makes a man or a woman". I guess it is like the saying "don't despise the small beginnings" – every one of us started with something small and over time it grew, matured and became something more significant and noble.

It is challenging and takes great effort to accomplish these small tasks, but if I can just change my attitude and my perspective, what a difference in can make in my life, and in the lives of the others I have influence over.

16

BREATH

"Sometimes it's the same moments that take your breath away that breathe purpose and love back into your life."

We talk about birth and life when the precious little one takes a breath, and cries. Then when one dies, we talk about taking our last breath. Life is measured in breaths, our first and our last.

The other night I was lying next to my youngest boy who wasn't well. His little face was so close to mine that I could feel his warm breath on my face. It may sound very strange, but I just loved the smell of his breath, the closeness – (when they are young, their breath is not at all offensive, strange but true!) One of my favourite things to do, is to lie next to my children and hear them breathe deeply when they sleep. To see their precious faces so peaceful and so perfect, and to hear that soothing sound of deep inhaling and exhaling.

I was overcome with such gratitude for life, for breath. It is so often that through my children, my Heavenly Father speaks to me. I need to slow down, stop and listen, to be still and wait.

Breath – it is something we take for granted, do you ever stop to listen to the breathing, the rise and fall of the chest?
We apparently take +- 18 000 breaths in a day – isn't that incredible? I never stop to think about it, but on this occasion I did.

Job 33: 4 [It is] the Spirit of God that made me [which has stirred me up], and the <u>breath</u> of the Almighty that gives me life [which inspires me] – Amplified Bible.

I want to live my life inspired by the breath of God, the Almighty.

17

THE DOING WORDS

Funny how when you leave school you think it is all behind you. Then you have children and must go through it all again by helping them learn, understand, plan and do the homework, study plans etc. The other day we were discussing verbs and adverbs in sentences. I was explaining the verbs as the "doing words" of the sentence and most often there are very few sentences that don't contain a verb. Even the simplest sentence "I am" is in fact true of this. So, we were trying to write sentences that don't contain verbs and it was quite challenging.

One afternoon recently, when we had the typical "I hate school" story and "why do we have to work and learn?" – this was while we were tackling a homework problem. So, I decided to do a little exercise of starting with the words "I am ..." to see how many positive things we can say. It was interesting, and I was aware of how quickly negativity can infiltrate our lives. But if we choose to speak LIFE in situations, the situation changes because our attitude has changed.

An example – my son said, "I can't do this, it is too hard", so he had to change the sentence to "I am able to do this. I need to try and do my best" – immediately the heart changed, and so the situation was not seen as hard and difficult. So often our speech is populated with negative verbs – such as "I can't", "I'm tired", "I won't!"

In this simple exercise I felt God showing me that this is true of His word too. I was reminded of these scriptures:

" Trust in me and lean not on your own understanding ...." Prov 3: 5

"Ask and it shall be given, seek and you will find, knock and the door will open" – Matthew 7: 7

You see, all these words require action, they tell us that we must DO first. God requires us to "do" and then He does. We must take that first step towards Him, and He comes to us. His heart is always for us. Throughout scripture, we are required to do our part and He does His BIG part.

18

TOUCH PAUSE ENGAGE

Being a South African, rugby is a part of our culture. I have watched many a game but still don't quite get the rules. I could, of course, make a concerted effort to understand, but just don't deem it important enough. I do, however know when to shout and scream, as you do, when the right team is about to score a try, but that's about it. I don't feel at all ashamed about this admission, but I guess I should be more open to things that don't really interest me – guilty!!

For those who know rugby well, in 2007 the scrum law was amended to a four step, "crouch", "touch", "pause", "engage" process, but now apparently, it is no longer used. Anyway, it always made me laugh as these huge, tough rugby guys would be about to tackle one another, when a little ref on the side line shouts the words, "Touch, pause, engage." Maybe it is just my sense of humor, but it sounded, and looked so funny!

I guess it is a good life motto though, as when one is in the game / battle of life (scrum) and facing opponents, to quickly reflect on those words, could really be helpful.

Touch – this could literally mean to keep contact with, or physically make contact with someone or something. I hope to always be in touch and to physically lovingly touch and be affectionate with my children. To also be in contact with people who are in this life game with you. Communication is very key!

Pause – take time to think before an action is required. Sometimes these pauses are very brief and other times they can mean a long pause – like a holiday. We always talk about thinking before speaking, so I think this is a good one to do too … to pause and breathe before reacting. (Not so easy when life is pressured, and impact is looming!)

Engage – this is a very active word as it means to physically encounter or make intention to, or to occupy the attention or efforts of someone. Life is full of engaging whether it's with people you love, friendships, colleagues and business. It essentially is the relational issues in life.

Rugby players are dirty and messy. They are dirty and messy, arm in arm, ready for action. This is such a good image of life – we are all players in this game of life, some grafting and fighting in the mud, others watching from the sidelines cheering on. No matter which part of the game you are in, there will always be a time when we all need to touch, pause and engage!

19

SIBLINGS

Our siblings are our first friends and playmates, our first rivals and competitors. This relationship is a long standing one as we grow with each other from babies into old age. Siblings ground us in ways that friends never will. They usually know the best and worst of us, and yet still stick together. Often siblings are our first role models in life, they are also our practice friends and can be our enemies too. Regardless, they are a gift and help us to be better, different and strong.

I am so blessed as I not only love my brother and sister dearly, but I also really like them — they are cool people to hang around with. They are both so talented, fun to be with and are nice people. They make me laugh, they "get me" and add so much value to who I am as a person. Of course, we fought a lot when we were small, but we always made up because we had too — we were in each other's space 24/7!

With my children, I constantly let them know that they are such a gift to us and to one another. To have brothers and sisters is very special and something they must always treasure. Recently we had a chat about their bickering and tried to show them that they have such special friends within their family unit – each other. They have learnt very important life lessons and will continue to do so, as they grow up. One such lesson is sharing (this is a biggie as in today's world, as life is all about ME and MY rights). In this family, everyone shares — we all share bedrooms (even mum and dad — hee, hee)! Share one another's clothes, share baths, share food and toys. Our lesson, which is constant, is that life is about preferring one another and not always doing what you want! This is very tough as we are all born selfish and the "SELF" of life wants to super-cede everything else, but as we mature, we realize that life is more about others. As a mother to these 5 blessings, I have learnt that I have had to become less selfish each day, to lead a selfless life by example. That can only bring about good, as I realize my life is not my own.

Another valuable lesson siblings teach one another is friendship. What makes the sibling relationship unique is that you are stuck with one another — throughout childhood that is. You can't break up, get divorced, or give up. We learn many social skills in families which we then take outside the home. A very important skill is conflict resolution. My children fight a lot but in this they learn to negotiate, compromise, to listen, to be heard, to win and lose, to apologize and to forgive — where else can you learn this skill set?

I want for my children to love one another unconditionally, to speak the truth in love, to always prefer one another and to be examples in life, speech and purity. What a better environment than to learn from young and to be a part of a family, and to have siblings who are in fact your closest friends.

20

CURIOUS

I just love curiosity in children. Where does it go when we grow up? It seems to morph into a "not so nice or pleasant term" called "nosey"! I guess curious seems to be the innocent exploration or searching for a reason or explanation. My two boys are especially curious – they pick up creatures and crawlies all the time and want to know what happens. For example, when an ant who has six legs now has two – how does it walk? So cruel, I know … the thing is they are not wanting to be sadistic or mean, but rather are just curious! (Those kinds of things, would never cross my mind – must be a boy thing?!)

I love a curious mind. It can be rather challenging when you must explain yourself, or random things in life to 5 enquiring minds, but rather they keep asking the questions and exploring, than to take life too seriously and at face value. How do you answer questions like?

- "Why do eggs come out of chickens bums?"
- "Why are elephants grey?" – I mean really – where did that come from? I never even think like that! They probe, question, challenge and keep my brain functioning on a very different level, so much so that sometimes I quickly dash off to go research on "google" their question.

To have a teachable, enquiring mind, and a heart that seeks is a good thing, yet sometimes it just takes faith to believe. Sometimes there is no logical reason, it just is what it is!

I want to always be "curious" for life, and when I don't have all the answers, that is ok too!

Who likes a "know-it-all" anyway?

21

ROCK PAPER SCISSORS

No matter the age, everyone knows "rock, paper, scissors". As we know, it usually gets played when one wants to win a bet, or get out of a chore etc. I don't know who invented it or even chose the 3 items – so random! I often see my kids playing it in order to not have to chore or fetch something for each other – you know how it goes? Why is it that the rock, seemingly the most sturdy and strong, gets super-ceded / covered by paper, and the paper can be cut by the scissors. Yet if there is the rock and scissors, the scissors loose as the rock crushes it.

The rocks in our lives need to be steadfast, strong, uncompromising – things that we hold fast in our hands, the un-changeable. The paper is often what happens to us in this life – we get 'covered' by life, it's stresses and strains- the busyness of life, the everyday mundane things that can cover our strong convictions, our rock-solid motivations. The scissors cut through the strains and may leave us depleted, broken, torn. In it all, our rock stands, it remains unmoved and unshaken. There are values we hold strong – solid as a rock – that are unchanging regardless.

THE ROCK I CLING TO IS JESUS. HE IS MY REFUGE, MY FORTRESS AND MY STRONG TOWER.

When I wobble with life and circumstances, I go to the "rock" who is unchanging. Right now, my children seem to use us, their parents as their rock, their refuge. That is not a bad thing, but as they grow and mature, we teach them to run to Jesus, the Rock of their salvation.

Our little family unit hold some uncompromising "rules" – they are what we hold close to our hearts and as they get older, they understand more and more about those values. Mostly they are unchanging and are strong regardless of what covers them in life and the circumstances that they face!

22

TENDER HEARTS

Last week we had a little dove fly into our home. I have heard that doves only 'nest' in places of peace? This made me chuckle as peace does not necessarily mean quiet, because our home is very seldom quiet! Anyway, we tried a few times to gently help it out the house, but it kept flying into windows etc. Eventually my son, who is fearless when coming to catch spiders, lizards, geckos etc., gently caught it, and we went outside to let it go.

Well, this little frightened dove flew back towards the house and landed on the ground, only for our dog to bite it and kill it!! All 5 kiddies went hysterical and I was screaming like a mad woman for our dog to let it go, but by then it was too late. I had to console all of them and the crying frenzy was deafening. My heart ached for these little ones who had to witness the cruel reality of nature. I couldn't protect them from it, but I could offer comfort and a very simple explanation. Our dog was no longer their friend for a long while after that. We buried the little bird and they made a tombstone, with flowers etc. It was a whole ceremony which was so cute. After the trauma, and prayers for the little bird, they all collapsed quite early that night.

I have always had a very soft spot for animals and I guess our children carry that too. Nature is in fact cruel on many levels and I guess it is like life. It made me realize that although we live in a cruel, harsh world, our hearts need to be kept soft and tender. A tender heart is a heart that is teachable, pliable and gentle. Gentleness does not mean weakness, but rather strength controlled. In this little life lesson, my children had to witness the instinct a dog has, which is to dominate or kill. I wish I could have prevented it, but it was too quick. They all immediately sought comfort in each other's arms and in mine, and in that I told them that no matter what happens in life, we are always here for one another and it is ok to cry and display emotions of tenderness.

May we always have soft tender hearts towards each other and our Heavenly Father like it says in Hebrews 3:8.

23

TIGHT ROPE WALKING

We recently watched this fascinating documentary on TV about a man who walks tightropes. This guy does not use any safety nets or mats or harnesses to protect him, and he is so brave (or crazy!) He not only walks this tightrope unharnessed but also does the most bizarre stunts. Being someone who is not crazy on heights at all, made me get cold shivers when the camera shifted from the stunt artist to the ground below!! It is mind blowing that a person can place himself at such huge risk! The amazing thing also is that he draws such large crowds!

This great feat of tightrope walking requires immense concentration and balance. I have a tightrope to walk, as do you, called LIFE and more than anything it requires balance. Sometimes I give a little to the left because my children need some extra attention, then I counteract and give to the right because of other needs. A key to this extreme art of balance, is a taunt rope or a tight rope – literally! One cannot progress or move forward one step at a time, without the rope being taunt. Life is never static and perfectly balanced, but there is always a perfect tension that is needed for the effective act of balancing.

My perfect tension is Jesus – the anchor of my life. I will need to always walk this rope, but the less weights and burdens I carry, the easier the load to bear, and the less complex it is to balance. I keep my focus on the goal at hand and don't look down otherwise fear will overcome me. Instead my gaze is fixed on the end prize, it does not matter how many times I move to the left or to the right to keep myself on the straight and narrow rope, but as long as I move forward one small step at a time.

24

SHOES

For some reason, my 3 girls love shoes! Ok, I must confess, I have a bit of a shoe fetish too, so I guess they have inherited it from me! Guilty as charged … anyway moving on … I recently bought a pair of pretty party / church shoes for each of my youngest girls. They are adorable, were very reasonable (always a winner!) and they absolutely love them. They are not allowed to wear these ones to school as they just get messed, so these are those "special occasion or weekend shoes!" They love them so much that they sleep with them on, and once asleep, I gently remove them and place them at the end of their beds. Our one rule (for myself as well), is that when we get a new pair, we give an existing pair of shoes away. They know this all too well, so before I had even taken the price tags off the new ones, both gave me their "give away" shoes. We then decide who they want to bless … we have several friends and contacts with younger girls, so it is never hard to find a willing recipient.

Shoes can tell a lot about us! They were even very important in Biblical times – in Exodus 3:5 (ESV) "Then he said, "Do not come near; take your sandals off your feet, for the place on which you are standing is holy ground."

Ruth 4:7 The Message (MSG)" In the olden times in Israel, this is how they handled official business regarding matters of property and inheritance: a man would take off his shoe and give it to the other person. This was the same as an official seal or personal signature in Israel."

I find this so interesting, as why didn't God ask Moses in Exodus to take off his robe or his head covering (if he had one)? He asked him to take off his shoes. I believe that this was a sign of God asking Moses to leave his identity aside and be vulnerable and comfortable in the presence of God Almighty. Then later, in Ruth, the swopping of shoes signified a "signed" deal – it was a guarantee of a promise, an act of integrity. How things have changed! Not even a signature today seems to be enough to seal a deal! It makes me think why one person would walk around with only one shoe on and have some other random shoe of someone else ... seems most strange but in those days maybe it was an outward sign to others that you were a man of your word! It was physical act of the intentions of the heart.

Consider the athlete who knows exactly what brand or type of training shoe he or she may need for track, field or long-distance running; then a ballet dancer with her specific "worn in" points; or a wedding shoe, a pair of heels the list goes on and on. All these shoes we wear represent something about us, yet they do not make us who we are, nor define us. In some cultures, when visiting a home, one would leave the shoes at the door, and walk in barefoot. A lot of the time it is purely practical, but maybe this is symbolic of leaving our pretenses at the door, so we may be "real" and vulnerable. I quite like that!

25

HEARING VS LISTENING

I think in our home the question we ask most often is "Can you hear me? Then why are you not listening?" There is a big difference between hearing and listening. I know for sure that my children can hear perfectly. How do I know this? Well, they can hear the sweet or chocolate paper being rustled in the kitchen when they are outside at the other end of the garden. How they know that this is not a broccoli packet, I do wonder? Maybe it is a special kid's sense?! Yet to hear their mother's voice when she asks to clean the room or feed the dog, suddenly, they have hearing issues! So, my conclusion is that there is in fact a difference between hearing and listening.

Hearing is the sense by which sound is perceived; the capacity to hear or the range of audibility; earshot. Whereas listening, is to try to hear something and to pay attention or heed. So, it proves my point that there is a vast difference between hearing and listening.

Even as adults there is this inability to really listen to someone. I challenge you to take notice of how often you listen to your friend, husband or children instead of hearing "blah- blah – blah." I am trying to teach my children to listen, take heed and pay attention to what I am saying as I believe this is a skill that is almost "lost" today. But more than that, is for them to take notice of and obey the voice of God in their lives. If they can hear but don't listen, what good is that!?

So often people are consumed with themselves, their lives, their problems etc., but a great social skill is to learn to listen. To sit back, say nothing and let them talk! I have learnt from my parents to do that – to hear, to listen, and to obey. I want to be the kind of wife, mother, and friend who does listen, so that others are free and feel safe to talk to me. I want for my children to hear the voice of God in their lives, to listen to it (pay attention to) and to obey.

26

THE LITTLE THINGS

There is a beautiful quote," Love, is not the big thing, but in the million little things."

I really love this quote as there is so much truth in it. Our lives are measured so often only in the BIG things that get our attention, and not the thousands of small things we so quickly forget. As a mother, there are so many little things that give me such joy and pleasure. One such thing, is when my little guy wraps his arms around my neck and tightly squeezes me, and says "I love you", or he says "You are wonderful" – I guess he copies me as I often tell him how wonderful life is now that he is in the world! It just melts my heart and makes all the other frustrating moments of motherhood dissolve in one instant. Some other "little things" that make me happy are: hot showers, crawling into my amazing comfy bed after a long busy day (I love my bed!), the first bite of a meal when I am *hungry*, or waking up in the morning and feeling like I have had enough sleep!

I don't love my children simply because I gave birth to them. I love each of them because of their own "million little things", such as the way the oldest child, number one, is beautiful inside and out and has courage and strength way beyond her young age.

The way my son, number two, has an amazing imagination, is very funny and creative; the way number 3, is so demonstrative and loving, and is very motherly to her small siblings, and our surprise package (twins), number 4, who has the most infectious laugh and loves to sing, and then our number 5, who is tidy and loves to help and serve. I could write a list about each child, and the million things that make them so incredibly special and unique.

However, it is also the little things that can cause huge irritation or frustration. For me, in one day there can be a thousand little things that make me feel so completely exhausted, yet I know that I must rise above it all and count my blessings in the very midst of these very challenging moments. As much as I am inputting and training my children, I am learning about myself as I discover all my weaknesses.

The great encouragement is that even though I fail and am weak, my God is strong, and His power and glory is perfected in my weakness.

27

SERVANTHOOD

I have a confession to make ... I am useless at star charts! I have tried many reward incentivized charts etc. but have not had any lasting success. The basic idea, as you may well know, is to reward the child with stars or stickers for every chore achieved, or for favourable behaviour such as obedience. In our household, we start off well (maybe the first 3 days), as the stars are administered for the chores such as unloading the dishwasher, making the bed, tiding the lounge and so on. Then it falls apart, as invariably one little person or perhaps two or three little people, decide to "borrow" stars from one another and add to their own charts! Or I forget to give the star to the deserving child, so it invariably ends up being a joke!

I used to feel extremely guilty about this as I felt such a failure as this is one area I just don't seem to get right! I thought it would really work well for us, BUT it did not, and it does not! I have come to realize that sometimes it works for one home, but not others and that is ok too, and it doesn't make me a bad mom!

In fact, these star charts made my children the exact opposite of what I was hoping to achieve – it made them *only* do things or behave a certain way if there was a reward or something in it for them. This is certainly not the type of little people I want to raise or add to this already pitifully selfish world. In fact, we want to raise the opposite … children who are motivated by their heart, children who see and do and take ownership of something without there being any recognition or incentive – this is called *servanthood!*

How key this is to our lives as small people and big people. There is a song that goes "If you want to be great in God's Kingdom, learn to be a servant of all." In our family, serving is a very important lesson as it always teaches my children to consider someone else. Even as adults, we must constantly learn to serve. I don't think it is ever fully mastered, as we must serve one another in relationships, in business, in our governance, in church life, in private and public.

Far more than reward systems (as let's face it, there are plenty of those in the BIG wide world of life), I want my children to learn the value and importance of these actions from our marriage and our life (in no order):

1. Affection
2. Saying "I'm sorry"
3. Affirmation
4. Attraction
5. Time
6. Laughter
7. Respect
8. Faith conversations
9. The value of friends
10. Servanthood.

This is my life quote....

" *ROYALTY IS MY IDENTITY. SERVANTHOOD IS MY ASSIGNMENT. INTIMACY WITH GOD IS MY LIFE SOURCE* " – *Bill Johnson*

28

TAKING TURNS

I am sure that in every household or family, everyone has heard of the term "taking turns" – some get it and understand and others … well, can do the 'flop and drop', or 'weep in a heap' as he or she wants INSTANT attention, wants their own way etc. etc. In any normal day, multi-tasking is mandatory in this household. I have learnt to listen to different conversations – each ear hears a different conversation, one child may be on my hip, while the other is on the kitchen counter and yet another is hanging on my leg or sitting on my foot. It seems totally crazy (which it is) but that is my "normal"! Of course, there are days when I want to run to the hills and hum, but mostly I just learn to adapt and know that at the end of every day, it is normally MY turn. What I want mostly is peace and quiet! Not a big ask I don't think?!

Trying to get 3-year-old twins to understand that they may have to wait for a turn to sit in the middle of the car instead of by the door, or to have a turn at choosing a DVD to watch, or a turn to pour bubble bath into the bath – get the picture, is a CONSTANT negotiation of craziness. If I could have loyalty points for every phrase, I use such as "How do you ask?", "Just wait, it will be your turn next" or "Don't speak to one another like that" – I may just be the highest loyalty member – pity it can't be converted or redeemed for a spa treatment or a holiday hey?

Even so, taking turns is a very real issue, even in our adulthood as it is a vital social skill! Turn-Taking is a crucial social skill that people need to master in order to be proficient in a variety of social situations." This world is all about the instant and the "NOW", and what it tends to do is cause dissatisfaction, and a feeling of being hard done by, or an unfairness. This only hardens hearts and causes jealousy, nastiness, greed etc.

So, all these seemingly monotonous lessons we teach our children in the formative years like sharing, waiting for their turn, manners and so on, is exactly a preparation for the bigger world where these skills need to be mastered. They are VITAL social skills! Let's keep on, keeping on!

29

REFLECTIONS

We have a wall of mirrors in our home – all shapes, designs and sizes. Often in the afternoons, when we are seated at the dining-room table doing homework, I see reflections of the outside garden in the mirrors, or sunlight that bounces off different objects in the garden, but one reflection I love to see are the little heads I have seated around me, doing homework and the general chit chat of the day at school. At times, it looks as though there are at least 20 kids in the home with these mirror reflections and believe me often sounds like it too with all the noise!

I also sometimes catch my little girls posing in front of the mirrors, pulling faces and talking to themselves. It is both so cute and funny to watch. I wonder what goes through their little minds. I hope that they see beauty, not just because they are beautiful in my eyes, but more that they have beauty within them. They have health, they have family, they have courage, kindness and hope, but more than anything they are loved by their Heavenly Father completely.

We have a story we read to them by Max Lucado called "You are Mine" – it is a wonderful story of His truth which is simple and never-changing: "It's not what you have, it's Whose you are." It is a truth that the lovable Wemmick, Punchinello, hears again at the knee of his creator in this faithful, fully illustrated sequel to You Are Special. Punchinello's lesson in love will help you speak God's heart to the heart of every child which is You are special, not because of the things you have, but because you are HIS! These books are gorgeous and are highly recommended to any parent or teacher.

In today's world, we are so bombarded with falseness. We are faced with an on-going battle of what true beauty is. Is it only the reflection one sees in the mirror? As these mirrors reflect us in our physical form, my desire is for my children to look beyond that, to seek the deeper beauty that is long lasting. That what God has placed within them – the talents, gifts and dreams, but more than anything for Jesus to be evident in their every action.

"In a mirror is where we find a reflection of our appearances, but in a heart is where we find a reflection of the soul!"

30

REPORTS AND REWARDS

Only God Himself fully appreciates the influence of a Christian mother in the molding of character in her children – Billy Graham

We have come to the end of term 2, and a long holiday stretches before us. What a great feeling to not have to get children to school (usually in a hurry), or make and pack 5 lunch boxes, do homework, trips back and forth from the school, etc. etc. etc. My children are also delighted to not have go to school to work and also to have a break from sport, homework and schedules.

Another sign of the end of term is the report cards. This is when I get to see exactly how my children have achieved and what the teachers have to say about them. It is a reflection on the term gone past, and the progress and advances made. With having 5 children, I have 5 very different individuals to consider. I have learnt to read these reports with a sense of humor, and to not "sweat the small stuff". Mostly, they all get very positive feedbacks. As their mum, I am fully aware of all their weaknesses, but just as much their incredible strengths and characters. One thing I have learnt and am learning, is to never compare my children to one another – this is an ongoing lesson always! Even my twins cannot be compared as they are two completely different little people who were just born at the same time!

In the BIG picture of life, who really cares what you got for your mid-year exams in grade 6, or if you could skip or hop, but I guess these are all "benchmarks" for the next chapter / phase / development in life. As adults, imagine if we had report cards issued every 3 months recalling our failures, successes and mediocrity! Imagine having your lack of patience rating as below average, or your dedication to exercise as incompetent! How funny that would be! As someone wise once said. "Be more concerned with your character than your reputation, because your character is what you really are, while your reputation is merely what others think you are."

Teachers have such a vital role to play in children's lives. Especially in primary school as teachers are idolized. I can recall several teachers in my life who were role models and made such a difference to my attitude towards school. Teaching cannot just be a job, as I believe it is a calling. I am so grateful for the teachers my children have had – loving, caring and Godly people.

So, as much as I am always eager to see how my children have achieved, I am also at complete peace knowing that more than anything, I want them to reach their full potential, but more than that I want their characters to be whole. My dream and goal are for them to be what God has called them to be, and that could very well even be different to my dreams for them.

31

GOODBYES

I just love airports! To sit on a bench or in a coffee shop and watch people at airports is one of my favourite things. I get so caught up in the joyful greetings and heart-wrenching goodbyes, that I often forget time and feel like I am in a movie. My children are the same but as they have not yet travelled, they still get so enthralled by the vibe of the airports – the landing and taking off the airplanes, the meet and greets, the tear-jerking goodbyes etc. We keep telling them, "one day" you will fly in a big airplane and we will go to the nations to visit family, friends and to enjoy all the beautiful sights of this world.

This week I say goodbye to my sister and her beautiful family as they go to the USA for two years to study at an amazing school of ministry. It is an incredible sacrifice and one that will add eternal value to their lives and many others – what an opportunity and how very brave! I know in my heart that this is what God wants for them and when the dream was first mentioned, I knew it would happen. As a family, we have had many goodbyes over the years. Relocation, going and coming has always been on our "agendas". To step into the "unfamiliar" requires faith without borders. To start over in the sense of familiarity, building new friendships, new currencies, new politics, takes BIG guts.

One thing I know for sure, is that when you give up the familiar (or comforts as they might be referred too), God breaks in and does the extraordinary as He builds into our characters. This doesn't mean you need to move countries or nations, but maybe a heart change or shift needs to take place in order for Him to break in!

To say goodbye for a while, to my precious sister who I have loved with all my heart from the moment I knew she was going to be added to our family, is exactly that – heart wrenching! I have quiet moments of tears, yet I know that this is right. I have watched her grow from a little, bubbly, happy girl to a beautiful young woman who is consecrated to God and the calling on her life. I have had the privilege of seeing her strengths developed and so now to see her "give up" the familiar to be obedient to the call on their lives, is the most amazing blessing.

My children have cried many tears as they see their family and little cousins leave to go to the nations, but they have learnt a lesson so valuable – no school or educational institution will ever teach them. That lesson is to follow Jesus no matter where He may take you, to be obedient and to be courageous! Yes, it is hard, and it is without a doubt not easy, but in His word, He promises us – in 2 Corinthians 12 v 9 "My grace is sufficient for you, for my power is made perfect in weakness."

This goodbye is for just a short while in the greater picture of life. I am so very blessed to see them go, and do, and be what He has called them to, even though I cry many tears!

32

TRADITION AND CULTURES

A few weeks ago, my son had some homework to do in his life skills book about traditions and culture. He had to complete two worksheets on his nationality, his family tree and what are our traditions as a South African family. We had a lot of discussion about this as we talked about all sorts of traditions that families have – some good and some bad. In our family unit, there were only a few that we could think of immediately …

We decided that our "traditions" were in fact special moments that we make into memories and we could label it tradition. For example, our one "tradition" is to celebrate birthdays. We all sing the happy birthday song, the birthday person gets tea or breakfast in bed, and gets to choose their favourite meal for supper that night, dessert included. Another is that we celebrate Christmas in a big way – not by lavish presents, but by having a big tree that we all get to decorate, mince pies and coffee or tea after church, and then a wonderful meal that we all prepare and share, and usually games after lunch or dinner. We had such fun discussing all these special times and although they have become a part of who we are, they are not in any way what defines us. Our birthday's and Christmas time is about celebrating, hospitality, kindness and honouring.

The term "tradition" renders a Greek word that signifies "instruction that has been handed down." Tradition, on the other hand, evolves, it is established by habit or custom and it will vary in its character from place to place, and from time to time. Tradition is not necessarily wrong as they may be wise, expedient, accommodative, etc. The issue is — what attitude do we entertain when someone is practicing a tradition that differs from ours? So often, we can allow our family traditions or cultures to define us and we can become rigid and inflexible. The traditions can be superior and "box" in what is never meant to be restricted.

One year, however, we decided to celebrate Christmas differently and a group of us used all the money we would have spent at Christmas time, to bless an orphanage and its workers /

caregivers with lavish gifts, food and essentials. It was amazing, as the joy and satisfaction we received from this giving expanded our hearts in a big way, and my children still talk about it today.

So, if tradition and cultures take preference over what He has instructed us to be or do, then it needs to bow its knee!
Galatians 4:8 – The Message (MSG)

8-11 Earlier, before you knew God personally, you were enslaved to so-called gods that had nothing of the divine about them. But now that you know the

real God—or rather since God knows you—how can you possibly subject yourselves again to those paper tigers? For that is exactly what you do when you are intimidated into scrupulously observing all the traditions, taboos, and superstitions associated with special days and seasons and years.
Amplified version "But at that previous time, when you had not come to be acquainted with and understand and know the true God, you [Gentiles] were in bondage to gods who by their very nature could not be gods at all [gods that really did not exist] – traditions!"

33

ASAP - ALWAYS SAY A PRAYER

Part of our bedtime routine is praying with our children. The little ones often copy what we say, but recently they have wanted to pray "out of their mouth" i.e. say their own prayer using their own words. There are moments when I want to laugh out loud as they are so funny! This brings such joy to me. My little 5-year-old girl recently asked me how we must pray to God. I asked her how she talks to us as her mum and dad. She smiled and said it is easy to talk to us, and in that she realized that that is exactly how we pray – we talk to God our Father with ease and confidence as He is our Dad.

A few days ago, my 3-year-old son, wanted to pray for his special friend who was sick. He literally closed his eyes for all of 3 seconds and said, "Father, make him strong like my Dad, bless him, Amen." – I smiled as I thought how simple, how profound and precious. That is exactly how we must pray – a simple, powerful prayer full of faith.

So often we get religious about what we say, how we say it, even where and when we pray. All our Father wants from us is for us to commune with Him, to talk to Him. My children teach me how to be simple, true and full of faith every day. When they fall and hurt themselves, the first thing we do is pray, then kiss it better, then they want a plaster/band-aid! (Always in that sequence).

Another precious moment was when my other little one, lay in bed one night and said, "Lord, I am so tired, my toe is sore and Starla irritates me, Amen!" Well, I was in hysterics and smothered my laugh in her pillow. Of course, Starla quickly responded by saying "Don't tell Jesus that!"

There have been many very funny moments in our prayer times, but equally many sobering moments when I have heard my older children pray. I have sat with them when they have had to pray for friends, or for forgiveness and help for bad attitudes, or when they pray for other families who have had loss or hardships that we don't understand. Every day, just like being in a family, there are moments of laughing and joy, and other moments of frustration, anger and tears, but in every moment may we <u>always, always</u> remember to talk to Jesus — <u>Always Say A Prayer</u>!

34

THE C WORD

Recently, a friend and I were chatting about what we think are some of the keys to excellent parenting. We had a good laugh at our experiences and naivety before kids. Many thought patterns and ideals have certainly changed! Boundaries have moved, our thinking has grown, and our characters certainly been tested. When I look back over the years, I can honestly say, I have done some growing! One thing that has remained true and steady is my heart towards Jesus. This brings me to a key word that I have found to be an absolute in my life – in being a wife, friend, daughter, mother etc. – that word is CONSISTENCY.

When I think of a picture of consistency, I think of a huge oak tree. The oak symbolizes strength and endurance. For this reason, it also stands tall as the national tree of many countries such as England, Poland and Wales, because of its symbolism of strength. Oak trees can live in a variety of environments and live up to and more than 200 years. It produces a taproot as a seedling which allows it to locate water even in times of severe drought, contributing to its long life. Oak wood has many benefits for the life of the people. It can be used to adorn the floor, furniture and wall paneling. This type of wood is totally hard and durable. For me, an oak tree is my picture of consistency. It is strength, durability through all seasons – seasons of beauty, harshness, bleakness, seasons of plenty, seasons of drought. It remains strong as it has one main root which runs deep. It benefits others and adds beauty, shade and hope.

Consistency is a steadfast adherence to the same principles, course, form, etc. If you think of professional sportsmen and women, it is not just talent that has got them where they are today, but consistent training. Another example is salesperson's growth is usually consistent with his or her company's earnings. Consistency is so lacking in society today which results in a lack of commitment and loyalty, double-mindedness, immaturity, weakness and vulnerability to pressure or influences. Husbands and wives need to be united in their parenting! There is a saying that has been used in mottos, songs and phrases over decades – "United we stand, divided we fall". It is certainly, hard work there is no doubt about that as it takes courage, digging deep into the truths of His word, and endurance or stamina i.e. guts! In my brief years of parenting, I have learnt many things, but one thing remains foremost in my mind, and it is being consistent. This is one word that I want to apply to every area of my life.

I want to stand strong not because of who I am, but because of who HE is my life – to produce fruit, shade and beauty.

Psalms 1:1-3

"How blessed is the man who does not walk in the counsel of the wicked, nor stand in the path of sinners, nor sit in the seat of scoffers! But his delight is in the law of the LORD, And in His law, he meditates day and night. *He will be like a tree firmly planted by streams of water, which yields its fruit in its season and its leaf does not wither; And in whatever he does, he prospers.*"

35

COMPETITION

It really fascinates me to see how different each of my children are when it comes to competition. When it comes to food, we almost have to weigh it out to make sure that their portions are all the same! When it comes to races and competing, some fight to the end, others give up when they know they are not going to win. The challenging lesson in this, is to teach them how to deal with the outcome, whether they lose or win.

There is something about competing that can either push one above and beyond, or a defeatist attitude occurs. I really believe that competition is good and healthy, but I also know each person responds differently to this. No matter, the fact remains that life is full of competition. My children have to know that their security and identity is in what God says about them, and not on the result of the race or competition or test., or even how we feel about them.

So, the other day, I was playing UNO with my son who generally has a bit of struggle when it comes to loosing. We decided to play 5 games straight, and then whoever won the most games, got to have an extra chocolate. I explained to him before we started, that this was a game and that the hand of cards you are dealt, is not rigged but the key is how you play the game. It is about strategic card choice and how you use the right cards at the right time. It can look like you are ahead and are going to win, and then someone puts down a lousy card, and the whole game can change! We had a little chat about how life is sometimes like that. We have choices to make all the time, every minute of every day, and it is not so much the outcome that is important, but more how we "play" the game of life. During the games, we discussed how his different friends react to situations and I was able to explain some simple life lessons/skills that I hope he remembers and applies. I was so grateful for this little session of teaching him through play, so when there is a bad attitude that emerges, we refer to the UNO game, and he nods and smiles as the "penny drops!"

Life is not easy, let's face it, but our choices are what determines the response to life and that is what counts.

PS – He won three games of UNO, so had the extra chocolate – just as well as I don't need it !

36

GARDENING

Every Saturday, we have a wonderful young Malawian man come to help in the garden. The little kids love him as he lets them "help" him by sweeping and raking leaves, he squirted them with the hose when they wash the car and he is generally so pleasant with a lovely big smile on his face always. He has now gone back to his family for 3 months as he has not been home for four years – it breaks my heart that the family is torn apart like that. So, this weekend was our first weekend without Kelvin and the twins kept asking where he was – it was so precious. We got them all working in the garden, but quite honestly it doesn't look like there was anything done!

Michael was putting compost on the flower beds and preparing for our first rains (which have yet to come!). Levi kept asking what the smelly sand was for, and I had to explain that this special stinky stuff makes the flowers grow and be strong and beautiful. His little face was so confused as it just didn't make sense in his mind. How very apt this is, as sometimes the stinky, smelly things we face in life (in other words – trials) can bring out such beauty! I had to admit, yep, it doesn't make sense but out of tough times, trials and "stinky" things we face, it can produce amazing growth, and fragrance.

Of course, the compost is not the only thing that brings life, but also a good rain and watering. The watering of His presence in our life allows this growth to take place, producing strength, beauty and fragrance.

I won't bore you with the details of some tough trials we are facing, but I do know that God is our provider, our defender, our hope and our joy. My little girl, Tayla often during the day, bursts forth into song (she loves to sing) and her favourite song is "Bless the Lord O my soul" – He uses our children to teach us and so every time I hear this, we all start singing the song and in our home it reminds us to do just that – BLESS THE LORD – in our speech, our actions, our intent and our thoughts. So, each day I will rejoice in what He has called me to, despite the *stinkies* in my life!

37

SONS

We have two sons who are such a delight, full of fun, need lots of love and very firm boundaries! They are so completely different to my girls and have needed far more discipline. My relationship is also very different with them as opposed to my girls. When you're raising a son, it's easy to forget that you're molding a man. A man who will carve his own career, calling and become a husband and a father.

I have come up with 10 points of how I am raising my sons. Some days it goes amazingly well, and other days, well, not so well! I hope however that between us as their parents, and with the help of wisdom, Godly influences and good friends and loving families, we can raise these boys to be great men of God who love passionately and live with purpose according to what He has planned for them.

So here goes …

1. Listen patiently – so often I get so busy with all the demands and requests that I can often "zone out" and not listen to my sons. I hear them, but don't listen. Note to self – be more attentive, stay focused and give them both ears!

2. Be his biggest fan and cheer him on – don't make a fool of yourself and embarrass your boy but let him know that he is completely supported by you. You are watching him on the side-lines in his sport, or hobby and fully are present i.e. not sitting on the side lines, texting or talking on the phone while "watching him"! Encourage the commitment to the practices and discipline of the sport – this is key I believe not only for boys but also girls alike.

3. Tell him he is strong – my boys love to hear they are physically strong like their Dad. My littlest guy often says, "Look mum, I am super strong like my Dad!" and he gets such joy when we praise him. To appeal to their physical strength, as well as their strength of character is very important. I often tell my

boys that I love their strong arms in helping me carry groceries or when they hug me so tight!

4. Be tender with him – make sure he understands gentleness – this is not weakness, but strength. As my boys have three sisters, they are fully aware of being "soft" with them when they play. They must respect their sisters and treat them differently – but every now and then, they swat them! We are still working on that!

5. Play with him – interact on his level – play Lego, kick a ball, play tennis, or play Wii – all of this is shows him you care, as boys' "bond" over activity.

6. Pray for him – to pray for him and with him is a very special thing. I pray often for Godly friends, for wisdom and for his future – his wife, his career etc.

7. Build his character – I encourage the traits I want him to possess, and work little by little, day by day, to instill those – being domesticated is a huge blessing for his wife

one day too! I am so grateful to my mom in law for teaching her son how to help.

8. Have fun times – be silly – do funny dances, laugh at his jokes, spray water guns, jump of trampolines and have tickle fights.

9. Give him room – as he grows and matures, allow him some space (this is yet to come and so have not got there yet!)

10. Let him go – I think this must be SO hard! But that day will come, and if I reckon if I have a special bond, although it will change, he will always love me. I want to let him go with the assurance of my love and the knowledge that I believe he is ready to make a positive difference in the world.

38

SPRING

Spring has to be my most favourite season. As it is early September, we eagerly await our first rain. Soon the flowers start to bud and bloom, and everything turns green and looks healthy again. It is such a wonderful season as it represents new life, a new beginning and the weather is just glorious with clear blue skies, gentle breezes and fragrance. Spring also brings more social activities as the days are warm, pleasant and outside activities resume.

My children were in the garden this last weekend, trying to pick flowers for me, and there were hardly any. I explained to them that we are just coming out of winter where everything died as it was so cold, but we are almost in spring when flowers start to bud and grow, the grass turns green again and it is a good thing – a sign of life. My little 5-year-old girl says to me, "Why don't flowers grow all year so we can have them in our garden all the time?" Before I answered I took a few seconds to ponder this. I told her that there are different seasons namely Spring, Winter, Summer and Autumn and we spoke about the special things that each season brings. We spoke of Autumn with the beautiful brown and orange leaves that fall to the ground for us to play in. Summer when it is so hot that we swim, and we have lots of outside suppers, then Winter when we enjoy hot bubble baths at night, warm fires and hot chocolate. Then spring with the new flowers, warm days and new life.

In every season, there is something to be appreciated. I am not just talking about the physical seasons we experience in our weather, but the seasons in our lives. My hubby and I often try to recall life before children as it seems so long ago! We have incredible memories of just the two of us. Our life now is crazy, busy but also so wonderful with our added blessings. There are of course times (quite a few) when we long for those "BC – before children" days – ha ha – but one day, they will all grow up and leave home and we will wish for those chaotic, mad, noisy days again. I guess, in every season we have times and moments when we "can't wait" for the next season. I hear people often say that they can't wait for winter to be over, or they "are so over the cold"!

I love every season, as each one has its own special qualities and memories. I never want to despise the season I am in. I have many "wobble days" but my faith is secure in Him, and I take one step at a time, one day at a time (sometimes an hour at a time), a season by season, because there is beauty, life and joy in each one!

39

KINDNESS

Kindness must be one of the most amazing characteristics. One of the many things I love about my husband, is that he is so kind! A kind person is generally thoughtful, or considerate, warm hearted and loving. To be kind to someone can make all the difference in their day or in their life.

I was reminded of some acts of kindness that have come my way. At one stage I kept a gratitude journal. It in I documented everything that I had been given or how I had been helped in the first year of my twin's life. It was a very hard time for me and I had many days of tears as I felt so overwhelmed and alone. Without going into too many boring details, we had moved provinces in my pregnancy, and my "comfort" areas, such as friends and family were not close by. I needed to write in this journal every day of all the blessings and acts of kindness I experienced in that time, as it helped me to focus on all the many blessings in my life instead of the loneliness and some very dark days. I came across it the other day, and many memories came flooding back. It brought tears to my eyes as there were so many special acts of kindness that I was and still am so grateful for.

Some of them that have deeply touched me have been ones that have been creative acts of kindness. A friend baked me a delicious chocolate cake and delivered it to me on my birthday. So often as mums our birthdays are overlooked as all the focus is on the kids, their parties, their cakes etc. So, to get my own special birthday cake was a great treat. Another one is, often when my Dad comes to visit, he washes up the dishes after a meal or clears the table. This act of kindness blesses my heart as it shows me, he loves me, as having a tidy home means a lot to me. Another is when my kids pick me flowers from the garden and place them in a vase in my room (I love flowers!). Another time was when someone (I still don't know who it was) paid for me to have a facial and pedicure. Then there was the time when a packer at our local grocery store, saw that I had 3 small children with me in one trolley and was trying to shop with another trolley at the same time (crazy

I know)! He firstly asked if he could help, and I thought how can you help me buddy? But he then took initiative and followed me around with the "spare" trolley, while I shopped for groceries. It was like having a butler! It was so incredibly thoughtful and brought tears to my eyes. I thought he might be wanting a tip, and quickly told him up front that I could not pay him for this help. He was almost offended that I had even suggested it as it was done out of his heart, and not because of what he would gain (which, sadly is often the motivation in our society these days). I could go on and on as I recall these special creative kindness stories.

I want to be that person who makes such a difference in someone's life every day. The person who is kind and considerate not only to those I love, but also to strangers. I want my children to make a difference in this world in a big way which is of course every mother's dream, but more importantly I want them to be the difference by showing acts of kindness in every situation.

40

WAITING

As moms, we all know that waiting is a lesson which is on-going with children. The younger they are, the more demanding and impatient they can be, and very seldom can wait for anything. In our home, if we are going somewhere exciting or fun, I almost have to tell them literally 10 minutes before we go, otherwise I get asked every 5 seconds how long it is till we go, and it can drive us mad! As the little ones don't yet understand time, I often must give them "markers" such as after lunch, or when my timer on my stove "pings". Recently, I have found this to work well, as they know that when the "Pinger" goes off it means action time. I have also used this to let them know when it is bed time or tidy up time etc.

My son mentioned the other day, that he can't wait until he is an adult, so he can eat chocolate whenever he likes and can stay up if he wants to. I had to laugh, as if life was that simple as an adult!

Waiting for the next best thing is also not such a great attitude as we also need to learn to be content for where we are at. It is, however, so wonderful having something to look forward to – like a holiday, or an outing, or something special. My husband and I try often to have little "dates" with our children where they each have their own special time with one of us. During these holidays, I took my eldest to a special place that she has been asking to go to for ages. We had a lovely morning painting ceramics, drinking hot chocolate and chatting easily. She told me in the car on the way home, that sometimes waiting for something special like this "date time" was better than having a holiday. It made my heart so warm and fuzzy, as I thought so often, we want to give our kids the very best and have these amazing exotic holidays, but it is the small quality times that can mean so much to them.

Being a big family, going on holiday is not an easy option because of logistics. There are many factors to consider, but we don't allow those things to stop us dreaming. As a family, we have dreams in our hearts of where we want to go, and how it will be possible, one day! We might have to wait longer than some families, but we are learning that waiting is part of our journey. The waiting itself becomes a prayer to God, as in this waiting to get in touch with the rhythms of life – quiet times, action times, listening and decision times. It is in the everyday things that we learn patience, acceptance and contentment.

41

HEALTH BENEFITS

We had a rough week last week with all five of our kids having a terrible gastro bug. I was reminded in this time of how important health is! I hate being sick and really am not a good patient. Through all my pregnancies I had terrible "morning" sickness, but it was never the morning but usually mostly afternoons and evenings! My last pregnancy with the twins, I was hospitalized with severe dehydration from violent "morning" sickness. So, when my children or anyone I know has gastro, I am full of sympathy as I know how awful it is.

In these moments of madness and exhaustion, I really do value being strong and resilient to sickness. It is something we take for granted so much and it is really such a blessing. So often we hear of people with huge health issues, children with incurable diseases and on-going immune deficiencies, allergies, disorders etc.

At the end of November, we are having a "Thanksgiving meal" with friends. It has made me think of all the many things we have to be thankful for. So often we are very quick to complain, and it has almost become the "norm" or default setting. I want to always have thankfulness on the top of my list. To be thankful for the daily things we take for granted – the ability to sleep through every night in comfort, to have food at every meal, to have a car to get me from A to B, to have children who are full of life, adventure, busy-ness and mess.

In Psalm 100:4 (The Message) it says "4 Enter with the password: "Thank you!" Make yourselves at home, talking praise. Thank him. Worship him."

To always to be thankful, changes the heart to have an attitude of gratitude. I know one thing I am constantly grateful for is health and its many benefits as it allows me to work, to help, to give and to serve!

"It is no coincidence that the first four letters in the word HEALTH are HEAL"

42

THANKSGIVING

Thanksgiving Day (Jour de l'action de grace in Canadian French) is a national holiday celebrated primarily in the USA and Canada as a day of giving thanks for the blessing of the harvest and of the preceding year. It is celebrated on the fourth Thursday of November in the USA, and on the second Monday in October in Canada.

This week we are having a group of friends over for a thanksgiving meal "SA style." In fact, 8 families! So instead of pumpkin pie and pecan pie, we are having baboetie, mealies, melk tart etc. We haven't ever done this before, so instead of a Christmas celebration to end off our year with our friends, it was decided that a thanksgiving would be a fun thing to do. All of us are bringing our best SA dish to share and we will have a time of fun, laughter and most of all a thankful heart.

In thinking along these lines, our family came up with ten things we are thankful for in our daily lives

– this is an unedited version direct from the mouths of the kids ....

1. Thank for being able to work and learn
2. Thankful for mom's yummy food to eat
3. Thankful for our nice comfy beds
4. Thankful for a car that has a seat for every bum (although squashed!) – this was one from the kids – no editing allowed!
5. Thankful for my sisters and brothers (even though they irritate me at times) – kid version!
6. Thankful for a swimming pool
7. Thankful for our family who live close by and some very far away
8. Thankful for my friends at school and at church
9. Thankful for my Lego
10. Thankful for strong muscles

Some of these pertain only to us as a family, but mostly there is always something that we can be thankful or grateful for. I have noticed that as soon as you start to focus on these i.e. having a heart of gratitude, something shifts in your heart and mind, and things don't look so bleak anymore.

When we pray at night with our children, they often say "We don't know what to pray." They now know that it is not about fancy words or the right way, but rather they need to talk to their Heavenly Father in their own little way and the best way to start when they "don't know what to say" is to start with the password "Thank you" – then the prayers go on and on and on …. thank you for my bed, thank you for my Mickey Mouse hat, thank you for my pink toothbrush …. you get the picture. But I would rather them start off with a thankful heart than anything else. As it says in the Psalm 100:4 – The Message (MSG) –4 Enter with the password: "Thank you!" Make yourselves at home, talking praise. Thank him. Worship him."

So as this week is a week of thankfulness, focus on all the many, many blessings that you have instead of what you don't have!

Remember the password – THANK YOU!

43

YOU GET WHAT YOU GET

We have this saying in our home which often helps to eliminate jealousy, comparison and fussiness. The saying goes *"You get what you get, and you don't complain"*.

Over the last few days, I have used this phrase quite a bit, and it is primarily due to the fact, that we are on holiday, and so the family dynamic is relaxed and very quickly the littles ones start to push the boundaries and see how far they go – but not with this mama!

It may sound a bit harsh or even a bit mean, but it does bring a bit of peace when they all start comparing the extra jelly tot / smarties handout, or the 5ml extra of juice one received (I mean really!) Amazingly, as I start the sentence, they all "chant" our little saying and there is very little complaining as they all know where they stand. There is an "almost" zero tolerance of fussiness in this family, and comparison as we all know is the thief of joy, so it sure isn't welcome here either.

I am guilty of complaining too and yet I catch myself often when I hear this saying going through my mind, and I instantly feel so repentant. Life, as we all know, is made up of choices, but there is also this factor of "you get what you get."

Sometimes life is not plain sailing and tidy, yet I am so incredibly privileged to be alive, to be healthy, to be able to work and earn, and for me the most important of all, is in my weaknesses that I turn to my Heavenly Father and trust Him to work in and through me to display Jesus in my life. I am a flawed human being (along with you) – true story! But despite this, I want to have a contentment no matter what situation I find myself in. This is also a great lesson for my children, as they watch and learn how I respond, react and apply things in my own life.

As we have a long holiday over Christmas and New Year, and just about every single person we know in Johannesburg has fled for the hills, or mainly beach, we are staying local for Christmas i.e. HOME! We have not had a holiday getaway at Christmas time yet, but despite that my children are perfectly content to be at home. There are times when the notoriously "baddie" of boredom appears but is quickly told to back off before mom freaks out! The kids need to learn to play imaginary games, to play with their siblings, to bake, climb trees, build Lego etc., and to accept that this will not always be our situation, but for now it is what it is, and you get what you get, and you don't get upset. Our life is awesome as we have one another and life itself is a gift!

44

MADIBA: CHARACTER + FORGIVENESS = HERO

It is only fitting that I write this one on Nelson Mandela who died a few days ago. He was a world re-known hero and the entire globe mourns his death yet celebrates his life and legacy! For every nation to acknowledge his contribution and for "small" South Africa to be talked about all over the world in different time zones, is quite something. The footprint he has left behind is something that challenges all of us to become someone better, yet it was only in his later years that his character was celebrated, and he became the famous hero icon that he is. As Wikipedia tells us … "Mandela was a controversial figure for much of his life. Denounced as a terrorist by some and called a Communist by his enemies, he nevertheless gained international acclaim for his activism, having received more than 250 honours including the 1993 Nobel Peace Prize, and others. He is held in deep respect within South Africa, where he is often referred to by his Xhosa clan as Madiba, or as Tata ("Father"); he is often described as "the father of the nation". Yet, before all of this he was a son, a scholar, a young man with great convictions, a fighter, a politician, a husband and a father, a prisoner, a president, a grandfather and a hero.

Our children will read and learn about him in the history of South Africa. The generations to follow will refer to him as one of the few great heroes. I have read that he was an incredible man of faith and humbleness. His life reminds me of Joseph in the Bible who went from prisoner to president, with many trials and hardships in-between, and many who misunderstood and disliked him. What I have learnt from Madiba's life is that although we all face incredible challenges, yet forgiveness is the key that unlocks freedom.

With all our challenges and frustrations in living in a third world country, I feel that there is no place I would rather be than in God's will, which for us is living in South Africa at such a time as this. My children are South African and have much to be proud of and much to learn from as our country is totally unique. Our rainbow nation has had a horrible past, there is no denying that, and the future is sometimes bleak and uncertain, but with the promises of God over them, they can make a difference. Yes, even one person can – look at Madiba!

So, one thing I know for sure, is that God is deeply interested in our character, not the titles we hold, nor fame nor gifting.

We have many who have fame among us but there are few who live a life worthy of honouring – that in my opinion, is my definition of a hero.

45

IPAD; IPOD; IPHONE; IDOLS ... I AM!

This year our older children are using tablets / iPads for their school learning. It is mind-blowing how quickly they adapt and learn. The education on these tablets is revolutionary and I only wish I had this way of learning when I was at school. Even the apps that are available from translating languages, learning times-tables, study tools, mind maps etc. are also completely overwhelming and so exciting at the same time.

I do however find it quite fitting that these items have a little letter in front of each item, which holds a lot of clout – the letter "i"! This little letter has become indicative of our lives – we live for self, kids are geared to seek their own desires and wants. Life is aimed at self always, yet we choose to live and be different. While I do admire all these wonderful tools that are available to us, I am also very aware of their subtle all-consuming influences, which if not managed are time thieves of epic proportions. The very thing that is supposed to help us run our lives more efficiently, and to be better at communication, seems to do the opposite and rob us and our children today of some very vital social skills and nuances, and having REAL "face time."

These little tools are addictive, let's be honest.

So, while these tools are useful and exciting, and are very much apart of our lives in learning, having fun and working – great discipline is required. We cannot run from the advances of technology and all that it offers, but we can master our time effectively so that we don't make these devices idols!!

In this busy life we lead, these devices need to be put away and turned off at some point, in order that I tune into the GREAT I AM. I have the "iAM" who is always available to me and never runs out of battery etc. – *He is the great I AM – the bread of life, the light of the world, the good shepherd, the resurrection and the life, the way, the truth, the life and the true vine.*

46

BUDGETS

This week, we (South Africa) had our annual budget speech presented. In a nutshell, SA's economy has grown although not as much as last year, the global outlook looks unsteady and there is a renewed focus on accountability and quality in education. Most households have a budget which is an outline of what and where the hard-earned money is spent. It is an estimate of income and expenditure for a set period. Most of us living in South Africa will agree that the cost of living has escalated a lot! Money does not go far these days and it is challenging to meet the demands of on-going price increases. Of course, as a family we know what we have to pay for each month, and where this money goes to, but in general I have a different view on budgets. So here goes (accountants don't freak out!)

"A budget is telling your money where to go instead of wondering where it went!" So often we are dictated to by our money! We allow words into

171

our vocab such as "I can't afford it", or "It can never happen as I will never earn enough" or "I can't be generous as I don't have anything left to give." I often chuckle when I hear people talk about their budgets, as so often in my life, I have not had a budget. You see, a budget can sometimes be a restriction or limitation as it can holds us back or prevent us from being who, and what God has called us to be – a budget smudget!

In God's economy, there are no limitations as we are to be generous and hospitable on every occasion, whether you have a full or empty fridge. (2 Cor 9: 6-15) I love this translation (The Message) *God can pour on the blessings in astonishing ways so that you're ready for anything and everything, more than just ready to do what needs to be done. As one psalmist puts it, He throws caution to the winds, giving to the needy in reckless abandon. His right-living, right-giving ways never run out, never wear out. This most generous God who gives seed to the farmer that becomes bread for your meals is more than extravagant with you. He gives you something you can then give away, which grows into full-formed lives, robust in God, wealthy in every way, so that you can be generous in every way, producing with us great praise to God."*

To use elements of the SA budget speech, this is how I translate into our family values and budget:

1. The economy has grown. An economy consists of the production, distribution or trade and consumption of limited goods and services in a given geographical location. Well, to confirm our Lloyd economy is growing all the time with limited resources! When I look at my growing family I sometimes get completely overwhelmed, but I am thankful that there is growth. Growth is good, even if it seems like nothing is changing, it is because it's growing and there is life!

2. Global outlook comprises two big and interrelated aspects: inclusivity and global relevance. It is also an idea of what a situation will be like in the future. I know my future is secure because I look vertically not horizontally! I need to lift my vision to be inclusive yet globally relevant – to be aware of the many needs that are in my own household and family, but to not lose sight of the

relevance of being part of the bigger picture! To teach my children to be closely connected to one another, but to know that they are history makers and world changers!

3. I need to teach my children how to have a renewed focus, which is to regain and reaffirm our values, our vision, our dreams and hopes for our family. It is to realign their focus to be on their Heavenly Father who can give them the desires of their hearts.

4. Accountability and quality. These two words are great and hold such depth and value. Accountability is answerability, as it is allowing one to give an account (be responsible for) their abilities or/and liabilities. So essentially it is the acknowledgement of responsibility for our actions. Being a part of a family, does exactly that. There is always someone who "will rat on you" i.e. find you out! This is a good thing as it doesn't allow for attitudes, sulkiness and bad behaviour. Quality is the standard of measurement or the degree of excellence of something. My desire is to raise our children with depth of character, quality

kids who love each other, and love others selflessly.

For my family, we have a budget – but it does not dictate to us how we give, nor does it control us. It is merely there as a guide.

47

#HAPPYDAYS

Sometimes we get so overwhelmed with our circumstance and challenges, that we forget to see ALL the good things we have in our lives that we can be grateful for. We forget how far we have come, what we have achieved, the battles (big and small) that have been conquered, as well as the million tiny things we forget to count as good!

A grateful heart is like a sponge that soaks up God's goodness. So often we soak up the negative and all that is going wrong in our lives and ignore all that we have going right. Life these days is not easy, everyone is super busy (whether self-inflicted or not) and consumerism seems to be at its peak. The cost of living, the rising expenses and many other factors contribute to people being overwhelmed with life. Relationships as well as raising well balanced and Godly children today, is incredibly challenging, and it takes effort, when our lives are already stretched in so many areas. But we have a choice as to how we respond to these circumstances, how we choose to prioritize our lifestyles, how we set the "big rocks" in place etc. One of these choices is having a grateful, happy heart.

Among the things you can give and keep are your word, a smile and a grateful heart. I am challenging myself daily in this, as well as to live unselfishly (well, as a parent I think that gets challenged from the get-go and continuously), and to not be too absorbed in my own struggles and busy-ness that I fail to recognize the blessings in my life. Our church has challenged us to this "7 happy days" in order to help us always have a grateful heart, which in turn creates a humbleness, and a thankful attitude as we acknowledge the many amazing blessings in our lives.

This week, while watching my three "smallies" do their swimming lessons, I could not help but smile at their enthusiasm to learn to swim. I was so grateful that I could be at every lesson to witness their growth as they enjoy this process. It made my heart warm and fuzzy! On another day this week, my son and I baked a chocolate cake and he "soaked up" this individual attention that we had together as we chatted over cracking eggs, licking icing bowls etc. It was a precious moment. Yet another, was when I helped style my daughter's hair as she was about to go to birthday party, and we casually chatted about friendships. These are special moments which I hope to never take advantage of.

Each one of us, adults and children, must realize that a grateful heart is a joyful heart, as it is not based on feelings or circumstances.
#7happydays

48

JUST KEEP SWIMMING

This last weekend, my two oldest children joined me in the Midmar Mile, which is the world's largest open water swim. It was their first swim and a momentous achievement.

As we were queuing with all the thousands of people, I felt quite overwhelmed with the responsibility of these two-little people. Of course, I knew that they could make it physically, but with any endurance race, it is often the mind that has to be the strongest! So as the horn blew, and we waded into the muddy waters, my son's face showed complete fear and nerves. My daughter started her swim and I told her to go ahead and do the best she can, as for us this race was about finishing and not about the time. So off she went. The water was incredibly choppy, and to try and get a rhythm going was impossible. There was a hectic crosswind and it blew us off course several times. Fortunately, I had my sister in law swimming with me and together we were able to coach him and help him across. But let me tell you there were times when I thought we are not going to make it! As his little 9 year body fought through these torrid waters, I could see his stamina and strength depleting, and most of me wanted to rescue him and tell him it is ok to give up, BUT I knew he could do it and more importantly I knew that for himself, if he made it across he would feel like a champ. A few times we had to calm him down, help him relax and breath, but he knew he had to keep swimming. I talked to him non-stop and felt more mentally exhausted than physical – it was that challenging! The chant in our head was "Just keep swimming!"

We eventually made it and wearily walked up the ramp to the finish line. It felt amazing to know that both my kids had finished, and me despite the most horrible conditions! (Soon after our race they cancelled all under 13 swimmers from swimming that day.) The life lesson in this swim was monumental for us all. So often we can "prepare" ourselves for life and think we are ready for what lies ahead, we can train, we can eat right and even mentally be strong, but when the rubber meets the road, or rather in this case, when the swimmer hits the water, that preparation can amount to nil! There was no opportunity to put one's feet down, or hang on the pool wall, or tread water comfortably as the waves just kept coming. Every breath was snatched away with a mouthful of water. It was uncomfortable and jolly hard and so often it felt like we had been swimming for ages yet gained no distance. Isn't that true of life, we forget how far we have come because we are so focused on what lies ahead.

This swim was so much more than a swim. It was a massive mental achievement for my kids. The fact that I was there right with them in the waves and crosswinds, and in the weak moments was a joy and a wonderful memory. It showed me how it is in our life, where God the Father is right there with us in the waters and in the hard swims of life. He takes our hand, keeps cheering us on, encourages us and gives us direction as He keeps us on course. Yes, there were some tears and many moments of wanting to give up, but to finish this was for me the best prize!

No matter what we face in our lives, through hard times, exhausting and fearful ones, crosswinds and big waves, He is with us – we have just got to keep swimming!

49

TALENTS

I love seeing the incredible talents in big people, but even more so in my little people. Each one has such a different personality, and as they grow up, I love seeing how they think and process life. Some talents are "on show" and many can admire them, such as a great singing voice, or an ability to paint or draw, or a great sportsman/woman. But there are also talents that are "unseen" and don't get a public vote. The role I play as their mother is very key, as although I want to encourage and help my children develop their talents, I also know that more than anything, their characters are fundamental to all that they are with or without talent. The character sustains them for the long haul!

When I look at my children, I see them for who they are, I love them unconditionally. It does not matter to me if they get the top marks on a test, or if they win a race or can sing beautifully. Of course,

I am proud of what they do achieve but it does not define my love or acceptance of them. What truly matters the most is their heart condition – how they treat one another, love others and show Jesus is all that they do. I am still discovering their talents as they grow and mature. I believe that some talents are deposited there from in the womb and others are nurtured according to circumstances etc. Whichever way, I love and accept them for who they are, not what they can or cannot do.

God's design includes the use of our talents. When God created the first man and woman, He gave them work that required the use of those gifts. He assigned them a profound task, much more important than anything you can accomplish in your lifetime. They were to take charge of the earth to rule over the world! But do you think the Lord counted them worthy because of their abilities? They had not even begun their work yet when he made his first pronouncement – He called them very good when they had not achieved a single thing. They had not proved themselves capable. He pronounced them good not because of what they had accomplished but because of who He had made them to be! Don't let the gifts or talents become your focus and consume you – as they become your master!

This is the right order of life – *the heart that knows the Lord as the source of beauty and value* and knows freedom. I need to remind myself of this in my daily life, and in all my epic fails! When I have a "melt-down" (and I do!), when I am strong and coping well, when I cry and feel weak, and when my day goes smoothly, and everyone is happy, I know that He loves me no matter what. I want this to be how I parent – to love my blessings when they are good, when they are bad and when they are darn right ugly!

This is my declaration for this year in how I love and worship Jesus, love my husband and love my children ....

"When your inmost being in in step with the right order of God, you reap His rest. Your soul tastes of His peace."

50

COMPARISON - THE THIEF OF JOY

Comparison, which essentially is the act of looking at things to see how similar or different they are. In a family situation it is not always helpful to have comparisons, as although it can be positive, often it is used to "show up" the differences or weaknesses of a person/sibling. It became more apparent to me the other day, when I was telling a friend about the differences and similarities between my children. It never ceases to amaze me how 5 individuals can be so incredibly unique!

Motherhood itself is full of comparison which can undermine and kill the joy of raising children. It is often what happens on the inside that can rob us of contentment and joy -such as how we wish we were that glamorous mom that always looks perfect, or when someone posts on face-book the fact that their 3-year-old is reading! How sad that one thought or statement from another allows us to immediately disqualify our achievements. To feel alone and inadequate is exactly what comparison does. It steals the very purpose and pleasure of life as it allows you to believe that you should be something else, and what you are doing is sub-par.

We compare ourselves to this person – the one who bakes healthy, organic goodies for her family in this gorgeous sterilized kitchen with perfectly manicured hands that are attached to her fit, flawless body that wears the trendiest clothes (that she bought on sale) which hang in her colour coded walk-in cupboard, where she prays for her family for an hour every day. Somewhere deep down we know she doesn't exist, but for unknown reasons we continue to hold her up as the standard against which we feel inadequate, insecure and incomplete. This is some version of a perfect mom, the kind of person we try and strive to be. But reality is that we are the type of mom that our circumstances, strengths and resources enable us to be. So instead of pursuing this image of a Perfect Mom, you're chasing after the Perfect You.

Some examples are that you read on Facebook that your best friend's 4 year old is writing the entire alphabet, and reading grade 2 readers –

immediately the thought creeps in of being a neglectful mom, because if you made time every day to write the letters, practice phonetics etc., your kid too would be reading and writing, maybe even in cursive or Arabic! Or if you see another friend who is gifted in craft ideas and always seems to pin these amazing projects that she has made with her kids on Pinterest, the same "bad mom" thought creeps in. I rarely plan fun crafts to do with the kids. Sometimes I feel so guilty about it and let myself think I'm a bad mom.

But I realize that I have different strengths and that is ok – I might not sew my own curtains or clothes, or have my children reading at age 4 or even 5, but I believe I have fun with my children and I want to help them grow up to be people who know God, and who deeply love and wholeheartedly serve God all the days of their lives. So, I focus on the things I AM good at. We bake, I sing and make up silly songs, plan picnic suppers, take them for ice-creams for no reason, write them special notes and put them in their lunch boxes and sing loudly in the car, and I make them laugh with my silly jokes and songs.

Of course, this does mean that I can't try to stretch myself and have craft time with my kids, but for the most part, I focus on my strengths and interests rather than trying to morph myself into something I'm not.

I want to choose to celebrate the differences in my children, as each one has incredible qualities and strengths, but also weaknesses. Together as a family unit we can help to mold, shape and develop weaknesses and strengths. So, as I try not to compare myself to other "perfect moms", I teach my children to be the best they are because there is only one of them and that is enough.

EXPECTATIONS

Learn to love without condition
Talk without bad intention
Give without any reason
And most of all, care for people without
expectation!

I just love this … I wish I could say that I do this all the time, every day to every person, but then I would be lying. Naturally, I have expectations, we all do if we are honest. That is what makes us human and of course "normal." Some of these I have grown in and am learning, but one area I do often fall short is the expectation part. Sometimes I have an expectation that people will respond to something like I do, but that is where disappointment sets in and often a hardened heart.

In all relationships whether it is husband and wife, friendships on all levels, parent to child, siblings, work colleagues, whoever, there is always a certain amount of expectation. This is good as it can create a boundary, a "safe place" of what is tolerated, or even what is predicted or allowed. I have certain expectations of how my children are to behave, and they have expectations of my role as their mother. For instance, they always know that they will be collected from school by me or my husband, that there will always be food at meal times, and so they are loved and secure in that expectation.

There is an expectation when two people love each other and say their vows, that no matter what life throws at them "for richer or poorer, in sickness and health," they will be there for one another and remain true and faithful. Life is full of disappointment, we know that full well, yet our expectation is that it will be good, and we fundamentally believe the best.

One thing I do know for sure is that when the waves come, and come they will, I have an expectation in the promises of what my Heavenly Father has told me. This last week, one massive wave hit us, and we had to steady ourselves and regroup! My expectation of my Father is that He is always for me, no matter how I might feel. When my head does not believe it, I choose to trust in Him and the promises in His word.

52

STORIES FOR HIS GLORY

One of my favourite things to do, is read. I love "escaping" into another world. My favourite reads have been autobiographies of people – stories of their lives, their challenges and victories. For me, some of the best preaches are from those who reveal God's plans and purposes through their own personal stories. Your own story holds so much credibility as it is your story – but more than that it often touches people deeply as it is real, the perfect drama with truth!

My children often ask me to tell them "stories from my mouth" which is in fact a "made-up story". So, the story from my mouth involves all sorts – bits about them, lots of imagination and sometimes I even get them to add to it and help expound on it. The look of their faces is just priceless, they are captivated and just love it. For me, as an adult, I also love people's stories – hearing their journeys through valleys and mountains, good times and bad, heartache and joy. We can all learn so much from each other and encourage one another.

God has given each of us a story to tell. I have many stories of life – its circumstances, the journeys (often some windy roads) and I know that I have many more to tell. I want every story to reflect growth, of how He has led me, but more how He has been glorified. These life stories are incredible and the stories I have of what God has done and how He has done it, has carried me and encouraged others. My children understand who God is, and they too can tell the stories He has added to our lives.

I have a story to tell, which is all for His glory!

53

BURDENS

Over the last few weeks, I have realized that I have been carrying too many burdens. Life happens, and circumstances allow us to tolerate and bear burdens without us even realizing it. I often make alternative plans and have plan A, B and C – and get myself in the way of God's perfect plan. During these so called "heavy" or tough times, I have heard a phrase too often and really don't like it – "God will never give you more than you can handle" is the phrase I'm referring to – what JUNK! The people who say it are speaking from caring and concerned hearts, BUT it isn't true.

I know that may sound harsh, but I promise I haven't suddenly lost my mind or have become angry but, when I realized the simple fact that God can and probably will give us more than we can possibly bear, it got easier and made sense.

I've often faced and am still facing trials that completely overwhelm me. So often my heart cries out a refrain of a song which has become my heartbeat over the last little while, and my anthem

… (It is well – Bethel):

"Through it all, through it all
My eyes are on You
Through it all, through it all
It is well
Through it all, through it all
My eyes are on You
It is well with me
Far be it from me to not believe
Even when my eyes can't see
And this mountain that's in front of me
Will be thrown into the midst of the sea
So, let go my soul and trust in Him
The waves and wind still know His name
It is well with my soul
It is well with my soul
It is well with my soul"

I wanted to know where that phrase was that people kept repeating to me in church and at work and over the phone, BUT I couldn't find that quote in scripture anywhere, because it isn't there.

It never mentions anywhere in the scriptures that the Lord won't give you more than you can handle. Yes, in 1 Corinthians 10:13 it speaks of Him giving us an escape from temptations so that it's not too much to bear. But when it comes to pain, trials, heartache, and burdens– not once does it say it won't be more than we can bear. Instead, it beautifully says this:

Matthew 11:28-30 – The Message (MSG)
28-30 "Are you tired? Worn out? Burned out on religion? Come to me. Get away with me and you'll recover your life. I'll show you how to take a real rest. Walk with me and work with me—watch how I do it. Learn the unforced rhythms of grace. I won't lay anything heavy or ill-fitting on you. Keep company with me and you'll learn to live freely and lightly."

The words struck my heart. My heavenly Father is speaking to me who is "heavy laden", carrying burdens much too heavy for my own shoulders. In that one verse He simply states the reason why we are given more than we can handle – it is so we can come to Him, so we can trust Him enough to hand over our heavy, crippling burdens and let him carry the load.

Besides, even He tells us that He is more than equipped and able to carry it, so why not hand it over? I have come to learn this and am still learning to hand it over!

2 Corinthians 12: 9 – The Message
"My grace is enough; it's all you need.
My strength comes into its own in your weakness.
Once I heard that, I was glad to let it happen. I quit focusing on the handicap and began appreciating the gift. It was a case of Christ's strength moving in on my weakness. Now I take limitations in stride, and with good cheer, these limitations that cut me down to size—abuse, accidents, opposition, bad breaks. I just let Christ take over! And so, the weaker I get, the stronger I become"

While I may be a strong person and think I can do things on my own and am "a tough cookie" – I cannot carry these burdens all by myself. I didn't really know how much I needed my Saviour and Redeemer, until I have no other choice. There have been times when things seem to fall apart, and times when I have choked on tears and many a time I have done "the ugly cry". Those are the times that taught me that Jesus is not just a want or a convenient symbol of love or a reason to do good deeds.NO!

He is the very air that I breathe, the reason that I live.

He is the only one who can make it bearable, when life is simply anything but.

Butterfly

204

54

BUTTERFLY KISSES

With just having celebrated Fathers' Day, it made me think of the richness I have in my life, as I have a Father who is a great Dad! There is no such thing as a perfect parent, but there are great parents, and he is a great Dad. He has always pointed me to Jesus – when he has felt failure and incompetent, he showed me how perfect our heavenly Father is. He has loved me unconditionally, he has challenged me and has allowed me grow. Even though I now have my own family and am "grown up", I still like to "bounce" things off him and get his wisdom and perspective – his opinions still count!

My Dad was always present – he was at every gala. athletics day and hockey match he could be at. He taught me life lessons and courage, he introduced me to the greatest book ever – the Bible, he taught me that the call of God was what mattered, and yet he never abandoned his family along the way, but rather took us with him as he pursued the call of God on his life. He walked me down the aisle and "gave" me away, and then performed the ceremony. I dedicated the song "Butterfly kisses", and we all cried, and still do when we hear it. He was there to dedicate my children to God – and is there cheering us on as we walk the road of parenthood. How rich I am!!

I look at my children, and often think how incredibly special it is that their father is so engaging in their lives – he cares, he sacrifices, he gives, he loves, and he disciplines. He is present and points them to Jesus despite all. What a legacy fatherhood is and what a legend this man is – the father of our children – my husband.

There is a famous saying "That anyone can be a Father, but not everyone is a Dad" – Dads are incredibly special to sons and daughters. To sons, they are their first hero, and to daughters, their first love. My children have such wealth as their Dad is present and he works very hard to provide for us, he is in apart of their lives and is fully present! He helps with Math's homework when their mother's brain is fizzed (cough cough!), he fixes the bicycles, reads stories and builds tree-houses. I am so grateful for him – an outstanding Father!

"Noble Fatherhood gives us a glimpse of the divine"

55

TRUST

Trust God from the bottom of your heart;
don't try to figure out everything on your own.
Listen for God's voice in everything you do, everywhere you go;
he's the one who will keep you on track.
Don't assume that you know it all.
Run to God! Run from evil!
Your body will glow with health,
your very bones will vibrate with life!
Honour God with everything you own;
give him the first and the best.
Your barns will burst,
your wine vats will brim over.
But don't, dear friend, resent God's discipline;
don't sulk under his loving correction.
It's the child he loves that God corrects;
a father's delight is behind all this.
Psalm 37 - The Message

Trust – this is a word that has challenged me BIG time, as for most of us when we quote scripture and say, "Trust in the Lord", most of us don't actually! Trust is the firm belief in the reliability, truth, ability, or strength of someone and that someone in this case is my Father God. I have been learning and will continue to learn what it is to fully Trust Him. In fact, I don't want to not trust Him.

Continuing from my last blog of "stories" – this is a little of my story over the last couple of weeks and it truly is a story for His glory in every way. To not bore you with details, we had to move and so began the tedious search for another home. Obviously, due to our above average family size, this was quite a challenge! In between our busy lives, searching for a home was probably, and I can say with confidence, one of the most stressful things especially when there is a deadline! We both saw probably about 20 homes and there seemed to be no hope.

There was however, one home that we had viewed right in the beginning of our search and although we both loved it, it was seemingly "out of our reach", but it ticked every box and more. Deep within my heart, I was hopeful but as time moved on, I had some wobbles and became very overwhelmed. I clung onto His promises over our lives and knew that He would make a way, when there seemed NO way. I began to dig deep and hold onto this scripture of trusting Him. Often, I felt God would say to me "Do you really trust Me?" and every day, this resonated in my soul "Who do you say I am?" It was a daily challenge, a daily walk (one step at a time) of saying YES! I do trust you, YES! I know you are El Shaddai (my shelter, my rock), Jehovah Jireh (my provider) and a God who never changes. Despite many people saying to us "it is impossible", we chose to not believe the negative reports.

Every night at bedtime when we prayed with the children, they would ask in their simple way "Father, thank you for our miracle home" – there was no doubt whatsoever that this would not happen! Child-like faith is priceless! It would indeed take a miracle as there just did not seem to be anything suitable which fitted us all in, and was in our price range etc. etc.

So, we continue to pack up all our stuff, and continued to search. The seemingly "impossible" home that we had seen in the beginning, suddenly became an option through a series of events that could only have been God. The Monday before we had to move on the Saturday (i.e. 5 days), the negotiation process started and only on Friday afternoon (the day before we had to move!!) did it get finalized. Friends and family were praying and every day there was anticipation "Have you found the home?"

We are now in our home and it has felt like home from day one despite the settling in process. We have been overwhelmed at God's abundant provision in our lives and this home is a blessing in every way. My children, at their bedtime prayers, now say "Thank you Lord for our miracle home. For all the extras and special things" – what a lesson they have learnt which they probably will only remember later in life, as for now it is "why are you so surprised?"

I am learning not to ever limit God to our circumstances, nor our paradigms, but to allow Him to teach me every day and in every challenge and in every joy, that He is the anchor and YES I do trust Him – His character is faithful and I do not lean on my own limited understanding, as I continue to give Him all the glory, and acknowledge Him in every way.

This is one of my stories for His glory!

56

#SELFIES

A daily selfie? Really? Did you think we forgot what you looked like 24 hours ago or are you just desperate for attention?

I might be showing my age here but have to have a little say about this crazy word, so here goes....

Everyone, well mostly everyone below the age of 30 knows what a selfie is, and isn't it telling that it is probably because SELF is so dominant in how they think and act. Of course, I am generalizing, but let's be honest, this generation that we are parenting – which involves training (an action word, or a verb i.e. takes effort) is far more absorbed with themselves than any other generation. In case you're unfamiliar with this term, selfie means "a photo that one takes of oneself, typically with a smartphone or webcam, especially for posting on a social-networking website." The term selfie is relatively new, only surfacing about ten years ago in Australia.

It has challenged me as although I don't take selfies, I am so conscious of how this affects my parenting and more than anything it has made me aware that these little blessings are facing life issues that we were not dealing with at their young age. We all know that children are very selfish, and they know three words very well – ME, Myself and I! Whilst we love to meet their every need and be a wonderful mother, we cannot always indulge them in their wants and desires. We have to go against the norm, and not spoil and feed that ugly beast of SELF.

Selfishness is such an isolating, horrible condition and narcissism is just plain problematic. Both these conditions prevent one from sustaining satisfying relationships as it is a total lack of psychological awareness, it is hypersensitivity to any insults or imagined insults, it is haughty and full of ugliness. Yet this very thing is in each of us. It is incredibly subtle as it creeps into our lives, our relationships and our influence of raising children with purpose!

One advantage of raising 5 children, is that there are not really any allowances for self. Bedrooms are shared, food is divided, outings are scheduled, turns are taken etc. – without realizing it they are learning the self is not the most important thing in the universe, but rather consideration and sharing is. In any successful and happy relationship, there is an element of "dying to self." Becoming a wife or husband, means compromising and learning to prefer one another, when parenthood comes our way, once again self is challenged like no other relationship!

So how do we do this – enable our children to be relevant yet not influenced by the selfie generations?

Here is my plan …
Galatians 5:16 The Message (MSG)
"16-18 My counsel is this: Live freely, animated and motivated by God's Spirit. Then you won't feed the compulsions of selfishness. For there is a root of sinful self-interest in us that is at odds with a free spirit, just as the free spirit is incompatible with selfishness. These two ways of life are antithetical, so that you cannot live at times one way and at times another way according to how

you feel on any given day. Why don't you choose to be led by the Spirit and so escape the erratic compulsions of a law-dominated existence?"

It is a conscious, deliberate choice to raise children who are not selfish little darlings i.e. BRATS! It is hard, it takes massive effort and action, but what a joy to point them to Jesus even when we fail and fail, we will.

57

UP, UP AND AWAY

The movie "UP" has to be one of my favourite "kid's movie" – and I will admit, I even cried in it, a few times! It is a wonderful film, with characters who are as believable as they have tempers, problems and obsessions. They aren't your typical animated beings, but they are cute and goofy. Two of the three central characters are cranky old men, which is a wonder in this youth-obsessed era. "Up" doesn't think all heroes must be young or sweet, and the third important character is a nervy kid.

It begins with a romance as sweet and lovely as two children named Carl and Ellie meet and discover they share the same dream of someday being explorers. Ellie and Carl grow up, have a courtship, marry, buy a ramshackle house and turn it into their dream home, are happy together and grow old. The lovebirds save their loose change in a gallon jug intended to finance their trip to the legendary Paradise Falls, but real life gets in the way: flat tires, home repairs, medical bills. Then they make a heartbreaking discovery. Ellie dies before they make their epic journey, the one they have dreamed of since young children.

Maybe it is so believable as it is an animated version of life – the reality of life. We all have dreams, adventures to fulfil and places to go, yet sometimes life just 'bogs' us down and they are neglected and tossed aside. So often, these dreams do not become reality as they seem so enormous or unrealistic, so any attempt at them seems futile.

One of our "goals" when we were first married, was to travel and visit Europe, before we started a family. So, the year before our daughter was born, we had our one dream come true and we went to Austria, the UK and Paris – it was such a wonderful experience, and as the quote goes …

"Once the travel bug bites there is no known antidote, and I know that I shall be happily infected until the end of my life" **Michael Palin**

As baby one came, then two, then three (you know the rest), life has become a little more difficult to realize these dreams as life is not simple and cheap! Yet it is still possible, and dreams do still come true. (They may take a little longer, but we can't give up). Many people have said to us that we will never travel because with a big family it is impossible as it is SO expensive – but we choose to not believe that – as anything is possible, and with God of course it is possible.

58

CULTURES

Typically speaking, when one mentions cultures, in my mind I immediately think of different values, attitudes, customs and beliefs of people groups around the world. Having just recently experienced a different culture to ours, by visiting Canada and USA, I have realized that although we speak the same language (English), we are in fact so different. Different is not a bad thing, in fact it is quite fascinating, and I loved everything about it.

When we got back, my children wanted to know all about America and Canada – what they eat, what the homes look like, do they have pets etc. You see, in their minds it is completely foreign, as they can only imagine according to their perceptions are which limited, and based on TV shows, movies etc. There are so many things that I thought were brilliant and loved – after all it is First World! To experience all these differences such as Walmart, 5 guys, Taco Bells, Trader Joe's, driving on the other side of the road, the currency to name a few, was just so wonderful to taste and to see!

Culture does make up some of who and what we are, yet my belief is only one thing – JESUS – and this one belief unites us with many who have that same belief!

My culture can also dictate my customs / way of doing things which can be both positive or negative, yet it cannot super-cede or dominate the way in which I live. This also ties in with my attitudes and my values – I cannot have a culturally acceptable attitude or set of values that contradicts my belief. We can all learn a lot about each other's cultures, but as Christians we live as one in Jesus Christ. Living in faith together is more about not noticing gender, race, or culture. Living in faith as a body of Christ is about loving and serving God, period!

We had stories about what we did and saw, the food we tasted (and they loved hearing the food stories – go figure – excuse the pun!) What a joy it was to experience this, and my hope and dream is that they will too when we all travel again, as the diversity of culture is a wonderful education and life lesson!

59

DRESS UP

This has to be my kids favourite past-time besides playing outdoors, and it is "dress – up." Over the years we have collected little dress-up outfits as well as vintage clothes, old party dresses etc. There is such creativity that is involved in this and I love the fact that there is such imagination and play, even their accents change according to how they are dressed.

Over the last little while as I have watched them play one of their many games, I was reminded of "dressing-up/ putting on" the full armour of God in Ephesians 6 of the Bible. I have felt challenged, and in awe of the strategy of the order in which it is spoken of in this text. There is a sequence that the Bible talks of in putting on this armour. The battles we fight are not physical but spiritual, and God doesn't do things without there being a reason, a Godly pattern or order.

Ephesians 6: 14 Stand therefore, having fastened on the belt of truth, and having put on the breastplate of righteousness, 15 and, as shoes for your feet, having put on the readiness given by the gospel of peace. 16 In all circumstances take up the shield of faith, with which you can extinguish all the flaming darts of the evil one; 17 and take the helmet of salvation, and the sword of the Spirit, which is the word of God, 18 praying always in the Spirit, with all prayer and supplication.

1. The Belt of Truth

In Bible times, the girdle about the waist held together the soldier's garments, which might otherwise hinder his movements while marching or fighting. The spiritual significance is that God does not simply want us to point at the truth, but He wants us to wear it and have it wrapped about us. Not only does the belt hold everything in place, but it also serves to carry the sheath that holds the sword of the Spirit for ready access. Without Jesus – who is the way, the truth and the life, we are hindered in the battle.

2. Breastplate of righteousness

The breastplate was an important article of defense that protected the front torso and all the vital organs, especially the heart. It was often made of a solid piece of metal, but it could also contain numerous small pieces that were sewn to cloth or leather that overlapped much like the scales of a fish. These scales could number as many as 700 to 1,000 per "coat." When the sun shone directly on the armour, it could become very hot. So, to avoid being burnt, or even pinched, by the moving metal plates, the soldiers always wore a sturdy robe under the armour.

In other words, wearing the breastplate of righteousness is always in partnership with the robe of Jesus' righteousness. "I put on righteousness, and it clothed me" (Job 29:14). The only way we can experience victory in battle against the devil is through confidence that the righteousness of Jesus covers our hearts and that we are forgiven.

3. Shoes of peace

In the Bible, the foot is a symbol for the direction or "the walk" of a person's life. Having our feet covered with the gospel of peace gives us good footing / grounding in pointing people to Jesus, as our walk is watched closely.

4.   Shield of faith

The warrior's shield was his first line of defense. Usually made of wood or bronze, it was often big enough to protect the whole body when the soldier crouched down under a hail of arrows. Likewise, faith in Christ's blood is our first defense against the great accuser (Zechariah 3:1–5). The shield was not held loosely in the soldier's hand but was firmly strapped to his fore-arm so he could resist the attack of an enemy's sword without fear of dropping it. Likewise, we as Christians cannot afford to have a flimsy faith while in the heat of spiritual battle.

The shields in Biblical days were also often marked or branded with the insignia or name of the king to help soldiers avoid fighting their own in the confusion of battle. In the same way, when the flaming arrows of temptation come, we are to hold up the shield bearing the name of our King of Kings, Jesus. Through faith in His name, we can resist and overcome

5.   Helmut of salvation

Some Christians have "rocks in the head" from neglecting to wear their helmets. The purpose for this helmet of salvation is not only to keep out the rocks, but also to keep in the brains! Your mind should not be open to anything and everything. As we study and come to understand God's Word, there should be a settling into the truth " that we should no longer be children, tossed to and fro, and carried about with every wind of doctrine, by the trickery of men, in the cunning craftiness of deceitful plotting" Ephesians 4:14.

Your body has seven sacred openings from the neck up: two nostrils, two ears, two eyes, and one mouth. (Our biggest problems usually come from what enters and exits the mouth. This might be why the Lord gave us only one — see James 3:5.) Only in eternity will we appreciate how pivotal to each person's salvation were their choices concerning what they allowed to enter their minds through these vital senses. We must firmly strap the helmet of salvation in place and guard these "openings" to our souls.

6.   Sword of the spirit

The sword was the most common weapon in battle. An interesting fact is that the word "sword" appears 449 times in Scripture. The sword is primarily an offensive weapon. In fact, the sword of God's Word is what Jesus used against the devil and it also gave the beast of Revelation 13 a deadly wound (Revelation 13:3, 14). When Jesus said, "I did not come to bring peace but a sword," He was not saying that He, the Prince of peace, had come to start wars (Matthew 10:34). Rather, He was pointing out that the sword of God's Word has a dividing effect.

Several times, this sword is depicted as having two edges: "God means what he says. What he says goes. His powerful Word is sharp as a surgeon's scalpel, cutting through everything, whether doubt or defense, laying us open to listen and obey. Nothing and no one are impervious to God's Word. We can't get away from it—no matter what (Hebrews 4:12). The two edges of the Spirit's sword are the two witnesses of God's Word, the New and Old Testaments. It is also called a two-edged sword because it is to be used both against the enemy and for personal use.

In Bible times, there was no stainless steel. A sword unused became rusty, dull, and pitted. Swords were kept clean by frequent use or by honing them against a stone (the Rock of Ages) or another soldier's sword. "Iron sharpens iron" (Proverbs 27:17). Likewise, when we study the Bible with others, our skill in the Word is sharpened. This weapon never left a soldier's side even when sleeping!

So, while we do not fight physical wars every day, we are in a spiritual battle and our "dressing up" is daily and has great significance!

60

SO, WHAT MAKES A GOOD STORY

I remember in English creative writing how as students we had to create a story using either a picture, or a phrase, or choose other options that were given to us. The English Profs used to say, that a good story has a beginning, a middle and an end. It usually involves believable characters, emotion, possibly drama or suspense, a thread or theme, good vocabulary and grammar, and then a punchline / ending or wind-down. It also must have credibility. So, as my children say to me when they want to me "make up a story" instead of reading it from a book, "tell us a story from your mouth!" I think I have a good story (from my mouth) – a story to tell of a situation that went down this week in my home – true story!

I don't want to document every minor detail in this incident, but one thing that I do want to share is that this is real, this happened, and I am alive and well to give an account for His (Jesus') Glory.

The sad reality is that many people are victims or subjects of crime in our country, and most have a tale to tell. I don't want this to be another one of those, but rather to be vulnerable as to the raw emotions of my simple humanity, so that my Father in Heaven may be given all the accolades.

On an afternoon this week, after a long, tiring day and crabby kids in the back of the car, all I was focusing on was getting home, and in my mind working through what needed to get done before the day ended. Sadly, a complete opportunistic occurrence took place, where I was a victim, for a few seconds, and was on the receiving end of a potentially violent crime. As I drove into my driveway and into my garage, with the automatic gate almost closed behind me, a man opened my driver door and held a gun to my head. My first response in those split seconds was what the hell was he doing in my garage, you don't belong here! It seemed in that same instance, I knew and tangibly felt the peace of God, I felt the presence of God and it was almost as if I knew what to do and how to respond. I gave him everything he asked for – my beautiful wedding ring, my watch and my handbag (which as we all know as ladies is full of everything but the kitchen sink!) My three small children in the back of the car went silent, but I know it wasn't fear, it was the presence of God. While I was handing over these items, I held my keys in my other hand and remembered thinking I must push the panic button for the alarm, but didn't have a clue which remote it was on, so I pushed the one I could feel without looking down and giving this man an opportunity to panic – excuse the pun! Talk about multi-tasking on a high level of emotions! I managed to push the right one and the alarm went off. Maybe this jolted him and although he spoke to me and I answered back, albeit very calmly and politely, he promptly turned around and ran out my garage into a getaway car waiting outside my gate.

At that stage, I leapt out the car, pulled all three children out of the back, without remembering how that happened, and told them to go upstairs with their big sister to bath as they were cold from being in wet swimsuits. Again in a few seconds, it dawned on me the severity of the situation and how my life and their lives were in such grave danger. At that point, and only at that point did I suddenly physically feel the fear. It felt like a prickly vine trying to wrap itself around me from my head down. I know and recognize that fear as it has tried to take hold of me before. I screamed out – "In Jesus name I rebuke this fear, it will NOT take root, it will NOT prevail in this home nor in the hearts or minds of me, or my children – BACK-OFF IN THE NAME OF JESUS!" In that instance, I made a choice to NOT fear nor fret. Yes, of course I did get a huge fright, BUT I see the protection of God in it all, in every detail (the tiniest of detail which I have not here elaborated on.)

Our home then became a whirlwind of security people, police (in the droves), and dear and loved friends who made tea, brought supper and generously gave big hugs. The prayers of family and friends (near and far) were honestly felt, and I know that I know that my Father in Heaven was with me every second of this ordeal.

Some may ask why did this happen? I don't know why, but I do know that in every storm of life, in every situation He is with us – He never leaves us nor forsakes us (Deuteronomy 31:6 "Be strong. Take courage. Don't be intimidated. Don't give them a second thought because God, your God, is striding ahead of you. He's right there with you. He won't let you down; He won't leave you.") So, I also choose to not think about the "what if's" – but I choose to be thankful for what I do still have – my life and the lives of my children!

I am highly irritated that I have to go through the massive inconvenience of applying for new identity documents, bank cards etc. I am sad that my special wedding ring has been taken and will probably be sold for next to nothing, as well as a special watch given to me. But other than that, I haven't given it much thought, since then, and my children have slept through the night, no problems and there is no fear in this home! Thank you, JESUS, as I know that He has not given us a spirit of fear, but of love power and a sound mind! My mind is still and is at peace, because of my refuge in Jesus.

The bummer side of it is that some of my stuff was taken which cannot be replaced. The funny side is that my little girl Tayla said to me – "Why did that man want your bag and ring; does he want to be a girl!?" Exactly! The chop took stuff that was not his and although it was valuable, I know that it means nothing in comparison to life, and to living life without fear.

As it says in the Word of God (Revelation), that I have overcome by the blood of the lamb, and the word of my testimony – all glory to Him – my Redeemer.

To answer if this makes a good story? Well, regardless of what you may think, it is my story and it is all for HIS GLORY!

61

SNAKES AND LADDERS

There is something very comforting about playing the good old-fashioned games without any swiping involved or double tapping (i.e. tablet / iPad games). It's the use of all ten digits, sitting around a game board and counting each square, it is team work and strategizing if one can, but it all depends on the roll of the dice. As I was playing the game yesterday with my 5 gems, it dawned on me how our lives are kind of like a game of snakes and ladders.

During our game, of course there is always some sort of life lesson and in this case, it was about being good losers, as well as also not being too proud because in an instant, one can slide down a very long snake, back to the bottom of the board. Two of my children (who shall remain nameless at this stage) didn't want to continue with the game after having slid down 3 snakes. Another child kept boasting of his / her achievement in getting so far up the board, when at the next roll of the die, he / she came crashing down to be in last place! "It's not fair" – was the common phrase in this game, and it made me think of how similar life is. Life can very much be like a game of snakes and ladders. Sometimes it seems more snakes than ladders!

The key to this is to remain humble, teachable and to not be proud as we all know pride comes before a fall! Sometimes, we win and other times we take longer to reach the top of the game. The point is not always winning, but sometimes persistently and consistently climbing back on and keep going.

There have been many times and most likely there will be more (sigh!) when we (Michael and I) have slid down some very long snakes and climbed some very short ladders! Despite it all, we have learnt some incredible things about God who is our very source and life, and about one another and it has strengthened us in many ways.

Character allows us to finish __strong__ and leave a legacy!

Recently, in one of my chats with God, I asked Him why this happens – this one step forwards, three steps backwards. In an instant I felt Him smile and say to me, "My child, together we are doing the cha-cha! We are dancing closely, I hear your whispers, see your pain, feel your heartbeat. I am with you, I am holding you and leading your every step!" I felt such comfort at those words and I realize that to be doing this "dance of life" with my Father God, is beautiful, it has rhythm and there is no other place I would rather be.

He is holding me close, He is leading this dance, I just have to relax, rest in His arms and let Him take the lead. Isn't that what makes a couple dancing look so good, when one leads, and one submits and follows. I choose to relax, breathe deeply, listen attentively to His whispers, His heartbeat and allow Him to take the steps, in which I follow.

So, despite the UPs and DOWNs of our lives, our struggles, our victories – He is with me, leading me as together we move to this dance of life!

62

KEEPING IT SIMPLE

It always astounds me that although our lives are full of technology which has enabled us to supposedly streamline and ease our lives, it has in fact done the opposite – it has complicated it in many ways. Most of the time it seems our communication skills have deteriorated massively. Of course, technology has, and will always be amazing! I mean to send emails, have automatic dishwashers, washing machines, appliances etc. is wonderful and I am SO thankful to not have to do this all manually every day! So, there is my first point of thanks – to be grateful for automation!

In our busy lifestyles we have however lost something – we have lost the simplicity of life! Some of my peers run themselves ragged with their children – they are in the car ALL afternoon going from one extra-mural to another, and all at different locations, times etc. They are called EXTRA-murals as they are over and above i.e.

extra and therefore require EXTRA planning – let us not forget extra money, and a very valuable thing called TIME! Nowadays it seems to be the norm that we fill our children's calendars (which means our calendars) with EXTRA stuff! What happened to school sport, because after all school is no longer free as it was in our days, and so let us rather make use of the sports, culture and activities at the schools. I do however understand that there may be some children who want to excel and achieve and therefore extra lessons are required at academies or clubs for reaching goals and what not. Though, we (mums and dads) are to blame for our HECTIC schedules as we firstly create it, and secondly allow it and partake of it. What about children coming home from school and playing for 30 minutes in the garden – climbing trees, having a swim or eating an ice-lolly on the grass? Maybe a NO entertainment technology day or fast day is good such as no TV, no computers, tablets, iPads, X-box blah blah blah?

I am endeavoring to keep my life simple. My life is busy enough with my 5 children and their different needs, but I am not "buying into" this lifestyle of killing myself while raising children. I want to be able to stop and hear the birds chirp (when did you last do that?), I want to feel the breeze on my face and not the cold blast of the air-con in the car as that seems to be my second home. Our children learn best by our behaviour, and to be able to equip them to keep life simple and the main thing the main thing, is quite challenging yet very possible!

Here are my 5 ways that I endeavor to keep my life simple this year:

1.   We have already blocked off time in our calendar for family time away. Sometime where we are away together just the two of us, and other times when we have family holidays / getaways. We have put the "rocks" in place of non-negotiable slots, and so will plan and save towards family holidays locally.

2.   Plan, plan and plan. The more organized I am, the more I can cope, plan and allow pockets of space in between a busy school week. So, for example, I plan a two-week meal menu where I know what we are having for supper Mon to Fri for two weeks running. It seems anal, but it helps me plan and it keeps that part of my life simple and easy,

and it also helps with the food budget. Most of the time this does work and is a great help, but also life happens and so I need to also be flexible too. Another example is trying to keep the children playing sport on the same day to eliminate 4 different pick-ups times in the afternoons.

3. I have done a massive spring clean / chuck out. It has eliminated a lot of extra stuff and mess! An example is the volume of clothes in cupboards – i.e. they now have only +- 7 shirts and shorts to wear (the ones that remain at the bottom of the pile and are never worn have been donated to someone else). Any toys, books, puzzles etc. that have not been played with in the last two months have also been donated. So, our playroom, bookshelves, clothes cupboards and drawers are all looking neat, lean and mean! The choice that the kids then have to make each morning is firstly, simple because there is not an abundance of choice and secondly, it keeps mess to the minimum as everything is that much neater.

4. I am being intentional about how I spend my time. If I am doing homework with my children or watching their sport, I am doing just that! I am present in the moment and giving it my full attention, and not doing it while I am on my phone either talking, texting or on social media!!

5. I have looked at how I spend my time (time being the MOST valuable commodity ever). What consumes the most time yet gives me the least amount of joy?! I have decided to make some changes in my life that has given me freedom to be more involved in the things that give me joy, and where I know I am called to. I have also put up some boundaries to keep it that way and have learnt to say NO to things that drain me. Time is precious and valuable, and once gone can never be bought back. Time is more valuable than money. Don't let anyone tell you different. You'll only have this moment once in your life. Better use it wisely. You don't want to wake up some day regretting the things you didn't do.

So, in a nutshell – get back to basics, keep the main thing the main thing and KEEP LIFE SIMPLE! You can do it!

63

QUESTIONS & ANSWERS

Just recently, I have felt a bit like this little person stuck in the middle of a few unanswered questions. There are many times when I get bombarded with questions from little people, and it feels like I cannot keep up with satisfactory answers. They can be the most mundane and silly questions, and then in between that is a deep question like – "Why do you think God used a rib from Adam, when God could have just made woman all on His own?" (By the way, I had a good answer for that one!) At times it feels like my brain is having load shedding, and it cannot keep up.

I have had a few questions in the last little while that I have wanted satisfactory answers on, and yet haven't had any. I think it is going to go one way, and it goes the opposite, or it remains unanswered. Sometimes I think that is the worst, the unanswered questions ... because there seems to be no way forward, and there is also the lack of closure. I must arrest my mind and settle it, and that takes some quiet place where I can get on my knees and pray. Often it is when I am horizontal in bed about to sleep, as that is when head-space is a bit less manic. I feel I have had a revelation on this issue of unanswered questions, which I feel my Father God has been teaching me. I am always learning, as my default setting (like every child) is to question when one does not understand. It is the big WHY???

It is this ... *sometimes God doesn't answer us like we want Him to, but instead He gives us His promises.* I have had many questions (like all of us) and still don't have the answers and probably never will, but *I trust Him.* One example was when we found out we were having twins. You see, we had not planned more than three children, so when I was pregnant with number four, and then it turned out to be number four and five – I had a freak-out moment, an ugly cry moment! I cannot begin to tell you how massively overwhelming that was (and often still is). I remember the day like it happened yesterday – the questions I had, and the insecurity I felt at being able and "equipped" to do this was huge. There were many times when I questioned "why me?", yet I held onto His promises – He is faithful, He is with me and will never leave me, He is my comforter, my Helper, my Rock and my Refuge, I am not alone.

No matter what situation is "thrown at us", and the questions we may have, I know my God and what His promises are. His names alone steady my failing heart, He is an anchor in the storm, and an ever-present help in times of need. Of course, there are real feelings like disappointment, frustration, heart-ache, guilt etc., but when I truly look at Him and to Him, my situation pales in comparison! When I have unanswered questions, I choose to dwell on His promises, because that alone is the answer. I trust Him!

64

BRIBES OR INCENTIVES

This week is now officially the end of our first term – holidays are in sight – phew! It has been a very busy term (like every other term) and parents, teachers and pupils alike are so relieved that the end is near. Reports have been issued and teacher feedback has been given.

We generally don't have huge expectations for our children, but we do know if they have not met the necessary criteria (obviously) and we know what their potential is, therefore there are some "markers" of possibly achieving more, and of course to always do their best. We gave our son an incentive (not a bribe, there is a big difference!) this year, and he met it. More than anything, he was so proud of himself, and I know that he now sees what we see in him – great potential! In his own words he said to me, "It feels so good to get great marks, as I have worked harder this term, and it is worth it now!"

So, you might wonder, "Okay, but what is the difference between a bribe and a goal incentive?" Bribing takes place when you offer something up front in exchange for good behaviour later. A child's right behaviour did not come out of a desire to do good but a desire for temporary gratification. Bribes pervert all sense of virtue, and children will respond to a bribe, but the changed behaviour will only last if the bribe has influence. You see, once the pleasure of a bribe is consumed, you are left with a behavioural vacuum. I know from first-hand experience, and yes, am guilty as charged. (Only the perfect parent hasn't EVER bribed their child!) You see, a bribe is temporary appeasement, with no lingering positive effects. (Just have to look at our government to see the results of bribes – CHAOS!)

Goal incentives are also offered upfront, not to motivate morally right or wrong behaviour, but to help a child achieve a developmental skill. Another difference between the two is found in the after affects. Goal incentives help establish life-long skills. Once a child learns to swim, get the best possible marks for their test or speech, tie a shoelace, ride a bike or play the piano, it becomes a part of his or her life. So, a key I am learning is this – Children should be rewarded for their obedience, not obedient for a reward. (Yip, hard to enforce and remember, but the long-term effects are SO worthwhile!) So, our son was rewarded for consistent hard work that has hopefully now become more of a habitual thing (developmental skill) – the feeling of accomplishment, after achieving and putting in effort – the "sowing and reaping" principle also plays a part here.

So once again, good parenting is hard work – it requires CONSISTENCY, which we all know is jolly difficult, but the long-term result is BEAUTIFUL! It has been said that a child who receives consistent reinforcement at home, will be a better student at school. He or she will learn faster because he or she possesses a greater ability to integrate and morally process. *ALWAYS STRIVE FOR CONSISTENCY in parenting!*

65

GOALS

I have had a few intentional conversations with some mothers recently, and it never ceases to amaze me how unfocused and confused some parents are. I asked one lady just out of interest a question – "So what is your goal for your children?" She looked at me blankly and replied, "What do you mean?" Gosh, then I was rather gob smacked … so we proceeded to have a conversation. The thing that astounds me is that most people have some sort of plan with almost everything in their lives. They would like to maybe be qualified as something, finish a degree or a course, own a car or a home, plan a holiday, go overseas and travel – you get my drift? Goals are kind of like dreams but with a bit more pursued interest, I guess. Usually, with having a goal all it means is that one is a bit more intentional about making the dream happen.

Well, having children is your biggest and most asset of all. After all, let's be real, they take A LOT of our time, money, resources, energy and focus, yet they are the most wonderful blessings. Having goals for raising a family is massively beneficial! It still astounds me that so many intelligent people 'waft' about in their parenting, allowing the little ones to dictate and set the tone – true story!

I am sure you are probably asking yourself so what is your goal smarty-pants?! Well, here it is …. it is based on the Bible and the scripture Luke 2:52 – "And Jesus grew in wisdom and stature, and in favour with God and man." This is of course a "broad stroke" goal, and there will be many smaller goals and plans that need to be tweaked and fine-tuned as we go along, but overall this is what our heart's desire is. We want to raise our children to be wise (having knowledge and good judgement) which is way better than being just smart! It is also to find favour with God (following His ways and seeking Him in all they do) and favour with man. For us as a family, that is our definition of true success – having favour with God and man.

I challenge you to have a discussion on what your goal is in raising your children?

66

STOP, BLOCK & TELL

I have recently been to an outstanding talk by Nikki Bush called "Tech Savvy Parenting." It was so informative and so helpful and full of great tips and "how to" tools. The overwhelming "unknown" that I have felt in raising our kids in this technology age is in fact not this massively scary monster. It is not all bad, it is not something to fear and therefore avoid. Common sense here still applies (like in everything, but then again common sense these days is not all that common anymore it seems!) The key here is to keep those communication channels open and have the little and big conversations – too many of us are not talking to our kids – this is not talking as in giving instructions or the "do not's" but rather having the meaningful conversations that they will remember, especially the "real" concrete stories – believe it or not, the kids still want the authentic. I hear many stories from my kids about their teachers experiences with spider bites, losing a child to cancer and a few others, which I know they will always remember (wish they could weave that into an algebra equation to help them remember – but I guess algebra gets used in SO many others ways every day of our lives – NOT!) (Math teachers, don't hate me!)

This phrase was talked about in the parenting talk – STOP, BLOCK and TELL. It is based on the firemen drill for safety – STOP, DROP and ROLL (if your kids have been to a real fire-station they will hopefully remember this). It was primarily a method to extinguish fire on a persons' clothes or hair without the use of conventional fire equipment. It is mainly a "safety mantra" that kids will remember and even adults in a scary or overwhelmingly dangerous situation. One must STOP (i.e. don't panic and get hysterical and stupid), DROP which is to get low, lying down if possible, covering their face with their hands to avoid facial injury. The ROLL is that the victim must roll on the ground to hopefully extinguish the fire by killing the oxygen.

The common-sense helpful safety mantra can also be applied in the cyber world and everyday situations:

1. Stop what you are doing if it is harmful to your mind, body or reputation. Don't get hysterical and panic

2. Block – if someone or something makes you feel uncomfortable or it is worrying you, block that person or game or website.

3. Tell someone – get help and talk about it – do not stay silent.

This is so true too of our everyday life in business, raising children, teaching children etc.

Stop it if it is hurting your mind, body or reputation. Bad behaviour, disobedience, deceit, unkindness etc. – STOP IT! Block those things that consume us and make us anxious and stressed. Or block potentially harmful situations like allowing your child to be friends with a kid that is known to be nasty or a bully. Block the 'stress' in our lives by making the right choice to eliminate the baggage that we so often create. Talk to someone if you are having problems or have concerns or doubts. We don't talk enough as we try to act like we have all the answers, meanwhile we are panicking inside.

Women are generally good at that – they talk often, and a lot! We can all help one another. I often chat to a dear friend who is ahead of me regarding ages of children, and so get her perspective and input and wisdom. Talk and ask – I do – a lot of it!

67

WONDER OR WANDER

English has to be one of the most confusing languages and so complex too. I am sure back in the dark ages whenever English became English, it wasn't supposed to be like this with past present tense, adverbs, false cognates, idioms etc. – it was just plain and simple, a language for communicating. Then someone decided to be clever and complicate it – a lot. Recently, I helped my kids with their exam prep, and while revising English my son asked me why English has to be so complex? Good question is it not?! I told him I don't have the foggiest idea, but someone thought they would complicate it and make it fancy and now we must be fancy too. (Maybe not the best answer, but I do have to agree with him.)

One of the sections we had to revise was "Confusing words" – and confusing they are. Let's look at Wonder or Wander – they sound the same, but that one little second letter changes it completely in definition. Do you know that there are over 250 confusing words in English – They are called false cognates because they sound or are written so similarly that they are often confused. I ask WHY? Why do we have to complicate things?

Recently, I have heard a lot of mums complain about how exhausted and 'stretched' they are due to the demands of parenthood, jobs, life etc. If one had to strip away all the "extras" life would be a lot simpler, and hugely liberating. So often, we are our own worst enemies as we create problems by over committing to things that actually are not really that important. For example, is it really necessary for your child to do ballet, swimming lessons, piano lessons, art lessons and playball? Come on, how ridiculous! Order your own world, and that of your children – it is not that difficult.

Life is for the living, not for striving. Maybe there was another clever person (like the English person) who thought that the more over-committed, and complicated life was, the more successful and fulfilled one will be. How daft! We are all guilty of filling our lives with unnecessary complications, but at the end of the day, no matter what the situation, remind yourself that you do have a choice! Choose wisely!

68

I CAN'T FIND IT

This is more of a practical write …

I don't know about you, but I seem to be helping my kids look for their own things a LOT of the time. I mean it is their own stuff that they play with or use regularly, and yet I am supposed to know where they put it! I guess in a way it is my fault, because so often they are amazed that I know something they did or said without being there and I tell them I am their MOTHER and so I know EVERYTHING! (So, in this case it's kind of backfires, but I won't tell them that.) Remember how Mary Poppins would click her fingers in the movie, and rooms would be in order and tidy in that second – gosh, how I wish I had that superpower! In fact, if I could add up and "bank" the number of minutes I have spent looking for things, then I would have a nice little reward fund for myself! (Note to self, maybe I should do this and charge them for every item I FIND – good thinking!)

Recently, I helped sort out the lost property at my twins preschool and I was stunned at how many items were there in the first place – I mean, really nice items of clothing and shoes, lunchboxes, hats, scarves etc. – it was mind-blowing that these kids (and parents) don't care or seem to even miss the items that are lost. I kind of wish I could have "shopped" in this basket of lost and clearly not really wanted items. It makes me realize as well that so often our kids have TOO MUCH STUFF! They don't need 16 jackets and 10 pairs of shoes! Firstly, their stuff gets so wrecked at school (especially pre-school) and secondly, they always gravitate to their favourites which are in and out the washing basket, so why bother? I have a word for it CLOTHING-BESITY! (That will be for another blog!)

Back to finding things ... so I guess in a nutshell, how do we teach them responsibility?

Here are some of my practical helping ideas (and I do use them, and they do work – not always immediately, but they work!):

1. Create a place where that particular toy, sporting equipment or puzzles live. For example, my 5-year-old son Levi, has colour

drawers for his toys. His red drawer is for books, blue drawer for toy cars aka dinkies and the green drawer is for Lego. The girls have a box for their hair bands, ties, clips etc. The art / creative stuff also has a box (yellow) where all paper, crayons etc. goes. The sporting equipment is kept in a wooden box so all cricket bats, hockey sticks, netballs etc. live there.

2. If they play with things and after one warning, stuff is not put away, I claim them. I put them in a box (hidden in my secret place) and they disappear for a while. This does take consistent effort, but hey that is what great parenting is – consistency! You know the scary thing is, most of the time they do not even miss that toy or book or whatever. So, if after two weeks or so it hasn't been asked for, I give it away – what is the point of keeping things that don't really mean anything to them anyway. (Of course, I am quite selective about how this works, but my children know this and so have learnt some hard lessons here!)

3. Don't always rescue them. For example, at night-time we pack the school bags for any extra-mural activities the next day. If something gets left behind, such as a hockey stick or shin-pads, don't take them to school, leave it. I know it is hard, as you want to help them, but the best way is for them to learn it through perhaps another source – not just mum bleating on about things – but maybe a teacher who moans at them or even gives them detention. So, what?! It is not the end of the world, and believe you me, they will remember next time! Mission accomplished!

As they grow and mature, it does get better and things don't get "lost" all the time! But helping create responsible humans is a mammoth, but equally worthy task!

69

FOCUS

I have two daughters who both wear glasses – each for different reasons. One for close work, and one for long distance. (I never remember the right terminology for near or far sightedness, so forgive me.) My younger daughter wears glasses due to a fall she had at 3 years old, and consequently it has caused some damage to her optic nerve. My older daughter struggles to see long distances and sometimes, while waiting for her after school I must "hoot my horn" to get her attention as she genuinely cannot see me parked a fair distance away.

I am often wiping smudges off their lenses, making sure the lens is clear and unscratched in order that they can focus and see clearly. There is something beautiful in this picture of how situations or circumstances can so often blur our vision, and we cannot see the detail in what He has for us right in front of us as such, and yet other times we struggle to see the long-term / bigger picture, the vision for the future, as we are fixated on the "blur" in front of us. Life has a way of causing our focus to become murky when things get a bit hard. If we choose to focus on the problems of our lives, those problems become MAGNIFIED! One small example is Emotions.

The truth is that we all know we have them (some maybe have a little more than others), but they don't have to rule us! When we choose to focus on the emotions, they get the limelight and are magnified. When we love what He loves, and hate what He hates, the vision is clear – no smudges blurring our vision and our focus.

70

RHYTHMS OF PARENTING

I recently heard a beautiful story of how motherhood is likened to a dance. It has its own structure and rhythm, and yet so often we want to dance someone else's dance, as we feel that they have the perfect rhythm and it looks so much better when they do it. The reality is each family has its own dance rhythm. Sometimes I feel like I am doing the jive – I bounce and weave all over the place to keep things moving and fluid (and can be left feeling breathless and exhausted), and yet other times I have felt the slow, steady and contained dance of waltzing in my mothering. Each dance is beautiful in its own way and in its own season. Imagine dancing the tango to Mozart – it just doesn't look good – right? My point exactly!

So often I can look at other families and think they have the perfect rhythm in their parenting as they make the dance look stylish, happy and fun. My rhythm is different to your rhythm and so comparison is detrimental to my uniqueness. Too frequently we compare our lives to others and in doing so allow insecurity or jealousy to creep in and pull one another down or make ourselves feel less valued. We all have areas we are striving to do better in, we all know where we need to change, and we mostly know what we can improve on (some areas can be blind spots though!) Sometimes I think I am not the "perfect" mother as I don't make play-dough from scratch (confession – I have done it, but it's overrated and MESSY), I can't sew, I can be very impatient and dislike mess A LOT! It is not to say that I cannot try new things or stretch and grow in areas that I may not be great in, but for me the character stretch and growth is more important than the achievements.

Think of how you are growing, loving, achieving, progressing. The role you are playing as a wife or a single mom or a widow, the child or children you are raising, the impact you ARE making, the home you ARE building. Think of the way you are mindful of others, generous and kind. The way you can make someone smile or laugh, or the way you can hug someone tightly and make them feel loved. Think about the fact that you are created by the

MOST HIGH GOD, and that you are known and chosen by Him. You are incredible, from your uniqueness to your complexness. If we all could just allow one another to be amazing and celebrate our own unique rhythms in our dance of raising children, our dance of being a daughter, wife, sister, friend, colleague etc., a lot of time and energy would be saved. So today, and every day I choose to celebrate others, to not be jealous or critical of one another and to appreciate and enjoy the rhythms of MY dance for His Glory.

71

TRUE NORTH

I am hopeless when it comes to navigating off a compass. My excuse is that I never was a girl guide! One thing I do generally know is my way around shopping malls – ha ha!! Most times, I still have to recall the silly rhyme I learnt in grade 2, to remember which one which is (sad I know) – Never (N) Eat (E) Silk (S) Worms (W). These are four cardinal points on a compass – North, South, East, and West. When reading a compass, and telling other people directions, I have been told to wipe "right" and "left" out of my vocab. Right and Left are relative directions and differ depending on your location and direction, but the cardinal points are constant. No matter the compass, one end of the needle always points North.

This last weekend, I heard these words in conversations of friendship – "We are friends, because we have a true north" – I absolutely loved this. It basically means that we can have many friends, each with different strengths, weaknesses, interests, gifting's and cultures, but one thing bonds us like no other, when we all have a true north. This true north is the moral compass of our lives, knowing and serving Jesus. I have some friends who are completely opposite to me and I often marvel at how much I love them, and how much fun we can have together, and I know it is because of our common "true north" settings.

My true north is always pointing to Jesus – even in my failings as a friend, my disappointments and expectations, my sorrows, my achievements, my mothering, my serving, my focus, I make my default setting ... my true north. You may ask, I don't know what my true north, is but I can tell you that Jesus is the way the truth and the life!

In my children's lives, while they are still small, I have encouraged (sometimes with a gentle nudging and other times a shove) friendships that are good for them. Friends, whose families share the same true north. As they grow and start to choose their own friends, that true north is set in them and they default and look for the same values.

I have some amazing friends in my life and my siblings are also my friends (that may sound like duh! but there are many families who are literally just that – family – and not friends!) I have friends that I know were "seasonal" friends and were in my life for a time or season.

Friendship is such a gift … *Proverbs 27:9 –The Message (MSG) "Just as lotions and fragrance give sensual delight, a sweet friendship refreshes the soul."*

72

PSALM 37 FOR MOTHERS

This scripture has to be one of my favourite. There are some vital words here that I hold onto in so many different areas of and in my life, and here is the how and why …

Psalm 37: 3-8 "Trust in the Lord and do good and dwell in the land and befriend faithfulness. Delight yourself in the Lord, and he will give you the desires of your heart. Commit your way to the Lord; trust in him, and he will act. He will bring forth your righteousness as the light, and your justice as the noonday. Be still before the Lord and wait patiently for him; fret not …"

TRUST – this little word is very weighty. I love how David (the Psalmist) writes this word first. It means to depend on God's promise for protection and support. How wonderful to parent and raise children depending / leaning heavily on God's promise of protection and support. Honestly, I do not know how I would parent / mother without my faith in God. In my mothering I need to confide in him and rest in Him. Instead of allowing my mind to be disturbed and sad and googling every conceivable behaviour or comparing to other mothers, I need to chill, and trust him that He has the answers. (Advice from others is good but choose who you get advice from.) I have a few good friends whose children are about 5 to 10 years ahead of mine in age, who have great kids. I ask them for perspective, wisdom and practical help, but my first point of call is Him.

DELIGHT – what a beautiful word. This word conjures up wonderful warm, fuzzy, happy thoughts and pictures – like rainbows, sunshine and giggles. To delight in my children and in life is a gift. It is not just being positive or up-beat when things are going well or when life gets tough, but it is rather having peace. Taking delight in the Lord means that our hearts truly find peace and fulfilment in Him. Does that mean, if we go to church every Sunday, God will give perfectly behaved children? NO! The idea behind this verse is that when we truly rejoice or "delight" in the eternal things of God our desires will begin to parallel His, and we will never go unfulfilled.

One reason why our life is troubled and restless is because of our internal struggles. It is not our changing circumstances, but our unregulated desires that rob us of peace. The very emotion of desire disturbs us as one desire unfulfilled is enough to make peace disappear! Some words that are opposites to delight, are displeasure, dissatisfaction and disappointment. Wow – many times I hear this in the conversations of mothers – and I am included. It is a weariness that creeps in and it robs us of delight and peace, when we think and expect our children to bring displeasure, disappointment and dissatisfaction.

COMMIT – well, this word means something slightly differently to what you first thought. It is not a pledge or a binding but rather a giving up of my cares, worries, burdens in everything small and big, my desires and necessities. It means rolling that big ball (and I mean this ball can be HUGE) of issues and stuff about not being a good mom, feeling guilt (we all know how guilt is so apart of us as mothers), exhaustion, anxiety blah blah blah away from me to Him. To give all my life unreservedly to God – yielding and looking to wholly to Him for support and guidance.

BE STILL – this is a super difficult thing to do as although my body might be physically still, my mind is racing by thinking ahead of 1001 different things to do, sort out etc. etc. To be still is not just a physical quietness but rather a deep soul stillness of not murmuring, not complaining (guilty of complaining!!) and to be content (another hard one). When thoughts come and feelings of shame, guilt and anxiety, I need to quieten my soul and be still by saying *BE SILENT, SPEAK TO THE HAND CAUSE THE HEART AIN'T LISTENING!*

DO NOT FRET – A biggie here for us moms! Do not fret / worry / be anxious / over-think / be constantly or visibly anxious as this is a kill-joy and it does gradually wear us down. Two words that are almost synonymous with mother is guilt and worry! Isn't that true? Well, my God who is the way, the truth and life tells me to not fret. If I can't listen to Him, then there really is no hope! True story! What does this mean? To not fret / worry / over-think etc. etc. means to NOT to do (no profound explanation but to STOP IT!) There are times, where I have literally spoken out loud to myself and said. "Enough, stop it now and give it up!" (I generally try do this only when I am on my own other-wise I may look a little

CRRRAAAZZZYYY!) It is powerful when one speaks it out loud – so in my own "chat speak" or "text slang" – SIOL – STOP IT OUT LOUD!

So, there you have it – my interpretation of Psalm 37 for mothers. Hope it encourages you as it does me?

73

FAMILY WALL

We have this family picture wall in our home that is full of framed photos of loved ones. Each photo has a special memory and many of them are of our children from their baby-hood to present day. I love sitting, looking at each photo remembering the stage or time that each one represents. The pictures are placed randomly and are all framed differently from size to a mix textures of dark wood, light wood, silver, gold, random colourful ones etc., and the gaps between each frame are not symmetrical. If I allow it, my OCD kicks in and all I can see are the irregular gaps and it can really bug me! When I choose to "zoom out" rather and look at the bigger picture of what each photo represents – the gallery of our loved ones and the memories each holds   the gaps don't even feature.

Just yesterday, I was thinking about my family picture wall and I felt God show me something in this. So often, I can focus on one thing and compare it to the another, seeing the imperfection in the way it may be positioned. The gaps between 'compartments/stages/phases/chapters' in my life can be very irregular, asymmetrical and sometimes non-existent. Yet the beauty in all these different phases, are for a bigger purpose. My life is like that, full of different moments, colours, textures and sizes – some bigger gaps, some smaller gaps and a skew picture every now and then. Sometimes, I must take a step back from myself, and allow my focus to move off the smaller irregularities of things, to see a beautiful, full picture. Of course, it does not mean that the little things in life don't count, because we all know they do, but it is choosing sometimes to take a broader focus at the whole picture and not each little imperfection or gap. This is not easy to do, and it can be a real struggle especially when I am in the thick of raising small children, BUT I cannot allow the imperfections to skew my bigger focus.

God is interested in all the nitty-gritty of our lives, and in every picture that tells a story and holds a memory. Sometimes, we need to step back, and look at the beauty in its wholeness.

74

PEACE LIKE A RIVER

We have recently spent a weekend in the Drakensberg Mountains in KZN. What I love about the mountains is the absolute peace – there is no traffic, no hum of the city or even other "white" noise. In fact, the first night we were there, my older son could not sleep as he said it was TOO quiet. How funny that we become so accustomed to "noise" in our lives that we don't know how to silence it or switch off. Peace is something quite rare it seems.

Isaiah 66: 12 "I will extend peace to her like a river, and the glory of the nations like an overflowing stream ..."

In this scripture, it simply means that peace will continually be with you just like a river is never-ending. It will feed you (support you) just like an actual river waters the plants on its banks and eventually the ocean. When your peace is like a river, you will never wither, and so you will always be producing the fruits of God's service. Your righteousness (in Jesus), will be never-ending just as the waves of the sea are always washing on the shore.

No one in their right mind would ever exchange "peace like a river" for "chaos like a volcano" or a "frustration like a Johannesburg traffic jam" and yet that sadly seems to be the daily experience for more and more families today. With the increase of 'screen time' in most homes, peace is not common. Peace does not mean quiet (as in void of ALL noise) but rather peace means contentment and freedom from disturbance. It is a stress-free state of security and calmness. So many of us live in an 'unpeaceful zone' – in other words – we live and accept that our lives are FULL of stress and in a constant state of insecurity and chaos! This seems to be the common thread in the 21st century for most families.

If I had to dissect what peace is and what it does to me, I would look at it like this. There is a conflict between two parties here: my flesh and my spirit, lies and truth, the fake and the real, the mask and the Saviour. Peace is that which stands between these conflicting parties and looks me in the eye and asks me permission to do what peace does best – *to give REST*. God my Father offers HIS PEACE to act as my umpire, to release me from having to be the authority and keep it together. But my part is that I must let peace be peaceful within me. It is a gift and all I have to do is receive it, but it is not always an easy thing to do. I have to choose to quiet the voices of the accusing party (the lies) and to allow peace to have the FULL authority, and LAST say. If I allow this, if I receive it, the peace of Christ will stand between me and the lies of the accuser, the lies that attack and bring shame and guilt. To let peace in and have it stay is indeed a mystery. I came across these statements in a book I was reading, and this is exactly it …

"You are free to be good because you are accepted
You are not responsible to have it all together,
You are free to respond to the One who holds all things in His hands
You do not have to live up to impossible expectations
You are free to wait expectantly on Jesus, the One who is both author and perfecter of your faith."

Philippians 4: 7 "And the Peace of God which surpasses (is greater than) all understanding, will guard your hearts and minds in Christ Jesus." THIS IS TRUTH.

So, don't OVERTHINK it, just accept it.

75

LIFE IN PICTURES

The other day I was searching for something, and I came across some old photos of our children as babies. Immediately a whole lot of memories came flooding back, and it made me smile and tear up all at once. Life seems to go by so quickly, and these "old" photos reminded me of what once was. Isn't it amazing how a photo can hold so much of a place or time or event (either good or bad)? Sadly, today we take loads of photos, yet they are all saved on a device, so the old-fashioned photo albums seem archaic as such.

I love learning from pictures and so I think I am a "visual learner." Even artwork can say a lot about a person or their particular "struggle" or "joy" in life. Artists will tell you that their most successful works of art have been those that were real to them i.e. the art represented something to them, and it wasn't just an arb object. Jesus taught us so many lessons using pictures in the Bible. One just has to read a children's bible story as the pictures speak so much more than the text.

Some examples:

- Jesus described us (His church) as a body. The body can hurt and be hurt (sometimes this is self-inflicted pain) and we can identify with that.
- The church is the bride – a picture of purity and beauty, a celebration of joy and love, and gatherings of family and friends
- It is a picture of family – father, mother and siblings. Each one has a different function and role to play. There are times of getting together, where it is chaotic and loud and fun (you know those family gatherings!!??) Yet despite all, families stick together through all sorts of life situations – mountains and valleys.
- It is a picture of a flock of sheep where Jesus is mentioned as the good shepherd. The shepherd leads and cares for his flock. He is concerned for each and every one.
- It is a picture of village – a community with different interests and functions, yet is seen as "one group"

- It is an army – it's about working as a team in the face of battle. It is not glam, nor smells like roses but more like sweat and blood. It is hard work – intercession and prayer are needed to stand ground.
- It is a building – a place of warmth, security and identity – a place for the presence of God to rest in us.

When we look at pictures it evokes in us many things – feelings, identity, joy, sadness or fear to name a few. Life is captured in pictures …

76

FINISHING THE RACE

My little girl recently had a "fun" Olympics day at school, competing in a few field events, and one of the events was a 200m race. I say "fun" because she didn't really find it fun, and although it wasn't supposed to be competitive, it was. She is not my athlete in the family, (which is ok) and she doesn't really like competing at any level (which I don't quite know if that is good or bad). Part of me totally sees her point of the "why do I have to do this when I don't like it?" But being the encouraging mother that I am, I made it out that she would be missing out on all the fun if she didn't go, as well as the BIG lecture about how sometimes we must do and participate in things that maybe we don't really like. (And boy, did I have many examples of that to share with her ...!)

Needless to say, she went with a good attitude (the MOST important character trait in any competition, opps sorry "fun" athletics day.) So we were there to support her, encourage her and tell her no matter what happens, or how she does, we LOVE her so very much and are proud of her even if she came last. Well, the one race, that's exactly where she came .... LAST. Not just a few milliseconds last, but really llloooonnnnggg seconds last. Shame .... my heart broke for her as she starting to cry and wanted to give up as she was SO embarrassed. One of her darling teachers, stepped in, grabbed her hand, spoke to her all along the way (as 200m is far for little legs to run) encouraging her and telling her she CAN do it. They ran the whole way and she FINISHED, and the crowd (children and parents) cheered. I was so emotional and very proud, even more so than if she had won the race.

This is like our life – it is a race / event, and some make it look super easy (those "natural" athlete types – grrrrr) and others trip, stumble or fall along the way. Some may be struggling at the back, feeling such failure and embarrassment, YET we have those moments where a friend/s comes along-side us and links arms, and breathes encouragement into our lives. We ALL need encouragement as we jog along in this race, but the most important thing and what matters most to our Heavenly Father is not how fast and slick we make it look, but rather how strong we finish, never quitting!

I love this in The Message Bible:

Hebrews 12:1-3 "Do you see what this means—all these pioneers who blazed the way, all these veterans cheering us on? It means we'd better get on with it. Strip down, start running—and never quit! No extra spiritual fat, no parasitic sins. Keep your eyes on Jesus, who both began and finished this race we're in. Study how he did it. Because he never lost sight of where he was headed—that exhilarating finish in and with God—he could put up with anything along the way: Cross, shame, whatever. And now he's there, in the place of honour, right alongside God. When you find yourselves flagging in your faith, go over that story again, item by item, that long litany of hostility he plowed through. That will shoot adrenaline into your souls!"

77

FULL LIFE OR BUSY BODY

I love this question and constantly ask myself this! This disease of being "busy" (and let's call it what it is, the 21st century disease of being busy, when we are never at ease) is so massively destructive both spiritually and physically to our health and wellbeing. It saps our ability to be fully present with those we love the most in our families and keeps us from forming the kind of community that we all so desperately crave. I mean we are even "too busy" to socialize and have "down time"! What on earth has happened??

Just one generation ago, the era my parents were born, there has been so many new technological innovations that we thought (or were promised) would make our lives easier, faster, simpler. Yet, we have no more "free" or leisurely time today than we did decades ago.

So, I must ask ....

- How did we end up living like this?
- Why do we do this to ourselves?
- Why do we do this to our children?
- When did we forget that we are human beings, not human doings
- Whatever happened to a world in which kids get muddy, get dirty, get messy, and heavens, get bored?
- Do we have to love our children so much that we over-schedule them, making them stressed and busy — just like us?
- What happened to a world in which we can sit with the people we love so much and have slow conversations about the state of our heart and soul, conversations that slowly unfold, conversations with pregnant pauses and silences that we are in no rush to fill?

All the time, every day, our standard greeting to one another is, "How are you?" But let's be honest, do we actually care, or can we even pause long enough to look someone in the eyes and really see if they are actually fine? Maybe I should rephrase that to ask, "How is your heart doing at this very moment, at this breath?" So, when I ask, "How are you?" I really do want to know, I really do. I am not asking how many items are on your to-do list, nor asking how many items are in your inbox. I want to know how your heart is doing, at this very moment. Tell me. Tell me your heart is joyous, tell me your heart is aching, tell me your heart is sad, tell me your heart craves a human touch. Examine your own heart, explore your soul, and then tell me something about your heart and your soul.

Tell me you remember you are still a human being, not just a human doing. Tell me you're more than just a machine, checking off items from your to-do list. Have that conversation, that glance, that touch. Be a healing conversation, one filled with grace and presence.

We are all busy, but busy is not a fulfilled life. Fill your life with that which holds more than just a "to-do" list. I want my kids to be dirty, messy, even bored — learning to become human. I want us to have a kind of existence where we can pause, look each other in the eye, touch one another, and be together and say, "This is how my heart is doing? I am taking the time to reflect on my own existence; I am in touch enough with my own heart and soul to know how I fare, and I know how to express the state of my heart."

So, I ask of you …. "Do you life a full life or are you a busy body?" Remember you are a human being, not a human doing!

78

BLACK FRIDAY SALES

Usually in South Africa, we are not too familiar with the amazing sales that are experienced in other parts of the world such as the USA. But for some reason, this year the marketing gurus jumped onto this band wagon and used it to gather crowds of shoppers to spend, spend and spend some more!

Everyone knows by now that Black Friday is the day after Thanksgiving, and the day in which retailers have huge sales on many of the hottest items of the year. Black Friday has become so popular that it has begun in some instances to usurp Thanksgiving, in that many stores, including Walmart, the largest retailer in the U.S.A, open on Thursday and begin their Black Friday sales on the holiday. The most commonly known story for the origin of the term Black Friday relates it to the black ink bookkeepers use when a company is turning a profit, that is, they are no longer "in the red." The traditional explanation is that the day after Thanksgiving is the time each year when most retailers finally show a profit, and that sales from that day until the end of the year are all Thanksgiving gravy.

There is something so amazing about human nature when it comes to sales. Regardless of whether the items or goods are needed, they are bought because they are discounted. I can be very guilty when caught up in this type of hype, although I really, really don't like crowds and the tension that goes with it. I would rather avoid the phenomenal sales because of the crowds. I think the psychology that goes with the sale purchasing is one of justification – "I can justify spending money on this, because I got such a deal / discount!"

So, I have given this shopping frenzy some thought and here is my view. Consumerism / Materialism has become so part of our lives that we can barely distinguish between want and need.

We all know according to Maslow's theory that there are only 5 basic needs for us complex humans, namely: basic needs (Physiological such as food, water, warmth and rest); Safety needs (security); Psychological needs such as relationships and friends; Esteem needs of feeling an accomplishment, and lastly the Self-fulfilment needs which is achieving one's full potential including creative activities.

The one huge "pull" we have in raising our children today is this overwhelming materialism.

- How do we put it all in perspective and live a life that is pleasing to God?
- How do we balance the wants versus the needs of our children?
- How do we raise them as considerate, kind, discerning people?
- How do we feed / grow kindness and honour, while squashing the monster of SELF / GREED / WANT?

This is all a process and it is ongoing, but here are some of our values and practical applications in raising our 5 gems:

- Whenever there is a birthday or event such as Christmas, we clear out all the unwanted, unplayed with toys or books and give them to others. There are normally charities that we give them to through our church and schools. It not only helps them eliminate stuff but the joy in the giving is priceless.

- We as parents have to model this well. We have to display in our lives a heart of thanksgiving, gratitude, generosity, kindness and selflessness.

- We need to hold lightly the material things in our lives but hold tight to the values and principles of our hearts.

- We need to have a conviction of how this looks in our household. We need to honour those who come into our home who have much and those who have little. Honour is a POWERFUL act (a Biblical principle) of holding someone in high esteem or respect regardless of how they act towards you, or how they are positioned. It is a heart attitude of submission. What gives HONOUR legs, is acts of kindness.

As this season of giving is upon us, may we display / model to our children the heart of our heavenly Father – generosity, goodness and love in ALL we do!

79

TWO QUESTIONS

I have been a bit quiet on the blog front due to a very busy November, but also don't want to just blog for the sake of it.

This month, I have had the incredible privilege of travelling to two continents – namely the UAE and USA. Both were so much fun, and my soul felt rich with experiences, opportunities and joy! The interesting thing was that I was two questions by two different people in two different nations which really provoked my thinking.

The first question – What is your passion?

Wow! I initially thought I could rattle off a whole lot of things that I am passionate about, but this is a much deeper question, which made me think A LOT! Of course, the obvious is that I am passionate about God – His word, His plans etc., and I am also passionate about my family. This person was asking rather, what makes me come alive and gives me energy. Maybe for someone who has a great talent or gifting, this is quite easy for them, but for me, not so much. I love writing, I love people but can also easily be on my own (maybe that is what happens when you have five children!), I love my church and my family. To answer more directly of what I am passionate about hmmmm .... I honestly can say this is still mostly unanswered. I love seeing people fulfill God's plan for their lives and seeing their potential become real and fleshed out. This is not as easy as it looks – you give it a try?!

The second question – What do you do for fun?

Fun!??? Another pause moment ... I do a lot of things that I know are good for me and good for my family yet maybe are not necessarily fun! (I hope that makes sense?) This was another deep thought moment, and so on the looonnnggg flights, and I mean llloooonnnggg flights between the USA and home, I did think a lot especially as the Charlie next to me snored for hours! So, I came up with a list of things I like to do for fun (especially when finances don't dictate!)

For fun I like to ....

1. I love to travel and experience new things / adventures
2. I like to cook and bake (but not always every day!)
3. Shop, shop and shop (I love bargains)
4. Spend time with friends socially, talk about the silly and deep things – times where I can laugh and cry in one conversation.
5. Be with my family – my immediate family (i.e. husband and children) and my extended family. I am so incredible blessed to like and love my family on both sides! That is really such a gift and one I never take for granted
6. I like to write, listen to music and have quiet time too (not too much of a big crowd kind of person)

So maybe, the next time you have a moment, think about these two questions, as they are quite thought provoking and quite telling too!

Give it a go! I dare you …. xxx

80

UNDERSTANDING

Assessing understanding might be the most complex task an educator or academic institution is tasked with. The challenge of assessment is no less than figuring out what a learner knows, and where he or she needs to go next. Just like a simple image demonstrates, our understanding is mostly locked in two bubbles – thinking and feeling!

Many times, after giving an instruction to our younger children, we say – "Do you understand?" I think for the most part, they might just nod and say they do, because they know that if they don't nod or say yes, it might cause more problems. So often for many of us, we respond like that to challenges. We hope and want to understand but based on our thought processes and possible feelings at that given time, we don't know if we do.

To be able to teach children concepts in education and for them to understand it, is in my mind quite incredible. As parents however, to help our children understand consequences to actions is also challenging, because so often we want to rescue them and make it easier, yet sometimes we have to take one small step backwards and allow a gap where possibly, the lesson can be the teacher.

This year, my daughter has been struggling to settle in school. The variables (from the friend dynamic, new routines, expectations etc.) at play in her little life is quite something. I could dismiss her emotions as immature (because she is exactly that, a little person who is growing and developing), but I must understand that for her it is a BIG deal. So, we have spent quite a bit of time just chatting through some scenarios and little issues, and if nothing else, I think I have made her feel "safe" to talk to me. We have talked and prayed with her and more than anything I want her to understand that she is loved regardless of how scared or overwhelmed she may feel.

For me, it just reminded me of how we feel as parents. We don't always know and understand how to do life and raise nice, normal humans. Often, we are overwhelmed too at the different variables that their ages throw at us, but I rest secure knowing that I can "talk" to my Father in Heaven who has promised me that if I ask for wisdom, He will not withhold it from me. This is the best wisdom, heavenly wisdom as it says in

James 3: 17 (TPT) ... "But the wisdom from above is always pure, [a] filled with peace, considerate and teachable. [b] It is filled with love[c] and never displays prejudice or hypocrisy[d] in any form and it always bears the beautiful harvest of righteousness! Good seeds of wisdom's fruit will be planted with peaceful acts by those who cherish making peace."

81

IT IS GOOD

So often we base the markers in our lives on how perfect and together we appear – or maybe it is just my observation!

Being "perfect" is a problem for women since we are more prone to perfectionism than men. Sadly, we don't just limit our determination to be 100% the best at everything to only one area. Instead, we want to perfect it all from how we look to how we raise children (striving to be the perfect mother – what does that look like anyway?) as well as trying to be the perfect wife, home builders, cooks, bakers or whatever we put our hand to. Women seem to be conditioned to spend their entire lives chasing someone else's definition of perfection. The perfect face without wrinkles or prominent features. A body without one dimple of cellulite! Have you ever met any woman without cellulite? The perfect entertaining skills, where you gather the twigs and leaves, you'll be gluing together for the table centerpiece prior to preparing a dinner from scratch for twelve. Doesn't everyone own a glue gun – especially a pink one???

Perfection though is overrated as it brings about an unrealistic, unattainable set of standards that are exhausting to maintain. You know those two words … HIGH MAINTENANCE … well that is exactly it! It is an unrealistic, never-ending dissatisfying end – it is maintenance at its absolute worst – ongoing with no break!

I think of perfection as the carrot on the end of a stick mounted to your head. You keep thinking you can grab it if you run hard enough, and sometimes you can get a little taste of it, but it's never enough. You want the whole thing, and even if you get that, right around the corner is another carrot waiting to be chased. You'll grow old and angry chasing perfection. So ….

- Wouldn't you rather look unique instead of like a mannequin?
- Wouldn't you rather be full of joy instead of perfect? When you have joy, everything is seen differently and not through the lens of perfection!

Six times in the chapter 1 of Genesis God declares what He has done as being "good". After man was created, He said it was "very good." Good is of course a positive term, but it is also a highly subjective term. If God says something is good, in my opinion you can't get better than that! What is good to me, might not be good to you. I could say Lindt dark chocolate is good, but you might not like it. However, if I said something was perfect that implies something else entirely. Here is the definition of perfect found in the Webster's dictionary:

being complete of its kind and without defect or blemish; "a perfect circle"; "perfect happiness"; "perfect manners";

So according to the dictionary, perfect means something that is complete, but not just complete, but something that is free from defects and flaws. "Good" (Hebrew טוֹב tôv) is used seven times in Genesis 1, and it indicates that there was no sin or death or pain. Sin, pain and death were only introduced after the opposite of good, "evil", was unleashed through the eating of the forbidden fruit. The first death was evidently the animal whose skin(s) God used to clothe the naked and shameful Adam and Eve. Prior to this God-initiated sacrifice to save people (foreshadowing greater grace and sacrifice to come through His Son Jesus).

So, in my opinion, perfect would imply something that could not fail or be brought down. If Adam and Eve were created perfect in a perfect world, it would have been impossible for sin to happen. Maybe God knew that man would be subjected to "the fall" and so He was not surprised at all? He already had a plan – a redemptive plan in Jesus. Since we all understand that they did sin, we can understand that they had at the very least, the potential for flaws. So, when God says it was good, what does that mean? I would say that in God's perspective or viewpoint on the event, He was pleased and was satisfied.

There is so much more to say on this phrase "it was good," from the book of Genesis, but for now I am concluding in the revelation that I don't have to be perfect. Good is enough as through Jesus I am made whole and He is the perfecter of my life.

This is one of my favourite scriptures ... Hebrews 12: 1-3 "Do you see what this means—all these pioneers who blazed the way, all these veterans cheering us on? It means we'd better get on with it. Strip down, start running—and never quit! No extra spiritual fat, no parasitic sins. Keep your eyes on Jesus, who both began and finished this race we're in. Study how he did it. Because he never lost sight of where he was headed—that exhilarating finish in and with God—he could put up with anything along the way: Cross, shame, whatever. And now he's there, in the place of honour, right alongside God. When you find yourselves flagging in your faith, go over that story again, item by item, that long litany of hostility he plowed through. That will shoot adrenaline into your souls!"

COST VS GAIN

Economists have told me that we may be on the verge another global recession. Although I did study economics at university and understood most of it (well I passed it!), I am still amazed at how quickly things can change based mostly on some bad decisions of someone somewhere.

The generally accepted – and rather broad – definition of recession is a period when economic activity declines. While most people agree with this, there is controversy over how to translate it into practice. (Don't worry, I will not go into a debate about the how's and why's of economic decline!) What I do know, however, is that it affects all of us in some way or another.

Most often, we make choices in our lives based on this little, yet massively weighty phrase – "cost versus gain". Think about the choices you make every day, such as buying groceries. If you are like me, I often compare brands, by comparing the costs and then decide. Or maybe you are not concerned with the costs, and regardless of how you feel or how much you want or must spend, you get it anyway. Lucky you! But for the most part, I am sure there are many people who "weigh" up the cost versus the gain in most of their decisions. Let's face it, money is involved in almost every decision we make daily, whether it is small or large. The sad thing is that this can also translate into our moral decision-making processes, such as how to discipline or raise our children, or whether to commit to something or someone, or to be a part of greater community. Allow me to elaborate... many times, the "follow through" processes of intentional parenting are so often too overwhelming that we cannot see the gain, all we see is the cost – the effort, the "fight". If I choose to dwell on this alone when raising my children, I have lost before I have begun. Complaining can so quickly become a part of our identity. I must choose daily, and yes sometimes hourly, to see the Calling of raising children for what it is. Yes, it is hard work (isn't no joke), yet it is exhausting and over-whelming, BUT the choice is that the GAIN far outweighs the cost. It is essentially about choice ...

- complaint vs calling
- exhausted vs excited
- hard-work vs honour
- grumbling or gratitude

It is not that hard really ... we just have to choose the attitude and approach. So even practically, when I look at the increasing costs of raising my family, I remind myself of the gain, make the adjustments and do the best I can.

I cannot allow the reality of the world I live it to dominate and dictate my commitment and calling in every area of my life. Regardless of the economic decline, the harsh realities of how that affects my world, I also just as quickly must remind myself that despite that, I belong to the King of Kings, and that is the place where my faith can flourish and grow.

83

THE WHY?

If you have children, you will know that this small three letter word can be THE MOST frustrating response to EVERY statement or question they ask. While at first, we marvel at their inquisitive mind and smile at their little questions, the novelty of it wears off VERY quickly. I think more than anything it is the perpetual asking of "why", as I am sure you have already answered the other 564 questions prior to that! I hear myself sometimes say, "Because that is the way it is or because I said so!" Yep, I am that mother who doesn't have an answer for every question beyond reasonable, and yes by that stage it is said in a rather irritated and frustrated louder than usual voice. In fact, it is quitting the question game, as I wonder what is the point and where is this going?

I am so aware of how overloaded and weary people are of late. Sometimes we are so tired and feel like giving up on certain things or are frustrated and unsure of what to do or where to go. The question asked so often is, "Why am I doing this? Why am I so tired? Why is this an upward struggle?" You see the real question we should be asking of ourselves is "Why are you doing what you are doing? Why are you carrying this load? or Why are you weary? Are you doing something out of duty or delight? Have you stopped seeing the purpose in all the responsibility?" Those WHY questions are not just seen as a negative, but rather they can help direct me and make decisions.

It is kind of like the saying that goes "keep the main thing, the main thing," – how often we lose track of that simple statement. We over think things to our own detriment sometimes, we over complicate it, we over-stimulate, and we over commit to things in our lives which should never be the MAIN thing in the first place.

It is quite simple … ask yourself and be aware of your WHYs – if you can't get clarity and it is so complicated, then also learn to say no and perhaps let it go or put it on hold until you can convincingly answer the Whys in your life.

A few simple examples:

1. Why do I bother with the difficult work of teaching my children values and principles? I do it because I love them. I could say a whole lot more on this topic, but for sake of simplicity, it is just that.

2. Why do I bother to plan my life and create gaps for our family to "breathe"? I do it because I see the incredible value in quality time, the investment and the great return of that simple task.

3. Why do we make Sunday a priority for our family to go to church? I do it because I love God my Father and serve Him with all my heart. To show my children the value of being a part of the local church is and will always be a core value and delight for us.

There may be some unanswered questions to the why, but maybe just the answer of "I said so" is good enough for now!

84

THE WAITING

As we have our school holidays, this first week has been one of catching up on some "admin" things. The one such admin thing was applying for passports for our tribe and renewing our own passports. It has been the one 'chore' that we have put off for so long since it is a tedious process and is not a pleasant experience generally. So, with our folder of documents, 5 kids in tow, off we went to queue, and wait, and queue and apply, and wait and queue again.

I won't bore you with the processes and details, but the interesting thing is that while queueing, conversations are had with all walks of life. I don't think we were very popular as our family of 7 took quite some time to process and we did "hold up" the queue quite a bit. I heard murmurings of "Jeepers, they have 5 kids!" The conversation in the waiting was interesting and it made me realize how people are so desperate to be loved and accepted. This one such lady, told me quite a bit of her story between getting re-married again, only being able to have one child, maintenance issues, family drama, travel and all while I just patiently stood behind her and gave her a smile. (This happens to me often, where I have random people pour out their life stories to me … I have learnt to see it as a moment where God can use me, so I listen and speak or respond only when I feel prompted.)

We are so often in a rush to get here, there and everywhere, that these moments of "waiting" really do speak to me. One cannot rush the processes or get uptight with the lack of efficiency or frustrated with the lack of systems in place etc. You just must wait, smile, be polite, listen and wait again. It was a lesson to me … do we make space in our lives to wait and listen? Do we allow ourselves to be fully in the moment, where there is no other option but to just wait and allow the process to unfold? I chose to not get on my phone like every other person in the room, but rather have conversations (well, this was mainly a one-sided conversation, but I was fully engaged in the listening process.) There is a beautiful scripture in the Bible, which so often I am reminded of, as I don't often do it …

Psalm 46: 10
I am guilty of seldom not creating space in my life to just be still. My mind races with schedules, meal plans, church life etc. and I allow it to crowd my thoughts when in fact, my Creator, my God and King is just wanting me to be still or in other words have some deep silence and calm, quietening all the stuff!

In the mundane chores of doing some admin, I felt my Father God speak to me in the queuing and waiting. I need to stop and listen. I need to create space in my life where there are no deadlines or schedules or things to be done, but I just be still and be calm in His presence.

85

THE TRAIL RUN

Call me crazy, but I decided to do this trail run on Friday night last week. It was cold and chilly (winter had decided to pay a little visit in Joburg), I was tired after a busy last week of school, and quite honestly did not feel like it at all, BUT I had friends running it too, so we were accountable to each other. So, I geared up, tried to pep talk myself and committed to doing it. When we arrived (in the dark), there was a pretty dismal turnout due to reasons mentioned above I am sure. I knew before I started that my head was not in it, and so it was going to be tough and very challenging!

We all raced off at 7pm with our headlamps on into the dark yonder on a golf course. Things look so different at night (well they don't look like much) as all we could see ahead of us was the bouncing headlights of those epic runners ahead, twinkling in the distance, and the uneven ground and trail we were running on. Literally, after 2kms I was justifying why I should give up at the 5km mark instead of doing the full 10km (it was two laps – argh!!) I was after-all, Tired and couldn't get a rhythm going and my breathing was not good. In my mind, I kept fighting the feeling of giving in, and at one stage I am sure I was talking out loud to myself, saying "You are a fighter, keep going, it doesn't matter how slow you are, just keep going. It is about finishing blah blah, pant pant, suck in air, suck in air ....!" You see the hard thing about running at night is firstly you can't see what lies ahead except where your feet land and maybe a meter or so in front of you. You also don't have folk on the side of the road encouraging you to keep going, neither marshals to guide you and give some little encouragement. There weren't even markers of how far I had come or how far to go. At one stage (after the 5km mark I am pleased to say), I looked ahead and could just see some bobbing lights and looked behind to see the same. I did feel a bit alone, and although I am not a scaredy-pants, I did feel a little vulnerable running on an unknown trail in the dark. I mean who likes running in the dark for "fun"!!??

I am pleased to report that I did finish, and I wasn't as slow as I originally thought I would be, but gosh it was an exhausting race! Sometimes, life is a bit like that. We don't have the energy, or the drive to keep going AND we have many excuses that are completely justified, BUT somehow one digs deep, so deep that we just manage to keep the steps going however slow or fast that may be. Sometimes, like I did, we feel alone. We can see that people ahead are exactly that, ahead and we feel like we are never going to catch up or finish. We see people behind and think, just keep going, they are pushing me to carry on and not get behind. All I had for company, was my ragged breathing and sounds of the night. But one good thing, at least I was still breathing and moving forward …. you see, life can sometimes be like that. We so want to do it better and get ahead etc., we want people to cheer us on and guide us by showing the way, but sometimes just sticking at it, breathing (however that may be for you – deeply, panting whatever) … the race of life is to just keep going and finish. It may just be a stage where you feel in the dark and alone, but it will pass, and it will finish, just keep going, one step at a time … slow, fast, limping however that may be!

Note to self … trail running not the preferred choice!

86

WHO'S THE BOSS

Due to the range of ages of our children, there is often this "pecking order" that occurs. The "pecking order" is the colloquial term for a hierarchical system of social organization and was first observed among hens! Well we have this pecking / vicious attacking order that sometimes happen. YES, our home is one that is NOT always full of rainbows, unicorns and sunshine! There is a hierarchal system between the children, especially as the personalities start to mature and can clash! The common statement is, "You are not the boss of me?" I am not too sure where that originated from as we (my husband and I) never refer to "bosses" in our home context. (It must be from school!) Anyway, I often must step in and say to the kids stop taking charge, it's not your place, we are the parents, not you guys! But of course, when age is on your side as a kid, those numbers hold a lot of weight when you want your own way or want to lay down the law in something.

They even say to us "Who's the boss of this house?" Both of us reply, without hesitation, Jesus is Lord and King of this house, which is even bigger and better than a BOSS! Somehow a "Boss" has such negative connotations attached to that little word. It conjures up feelings of resentment, fear maybe and even sometimes rebellion. There is a big difference to someone being the boss, and someone who is leading and put in charge because of their willingness to serve and love. In our home, as the parents, we are the "Bosses" of our little tribe, but more than that, we are leading our children in the ways of God (and we do fail, and we do mess up) but we have been given authority over their lives and so we need to lead them strong in the ways of God.

I find it interesting, that when children play the game "Follow my Leader", it is exactly that. One follows in the foot-steps of a leader, someone they trust and can follow. It is not called "Follow my boss" as often, one doesn't choose to follow a boss, one just has to do what the boss says, and there is often a lack of respect. Leading however, is different. Even in marriage when there is a "boss", all it does is create frustrations, intimidation and fear. When a husband leads a wife and his family (not at all in dominance or "lording" over her and them), there is life and a fragrance that is so attractive.

When we hear the statement "You not the boss of me!" – it reminds us all that we live to serve one another and have Jesus reign in our lives not because of fear, but because where good leadership is, there is growth, security, life and fragrance!

87

TO BE KIND

Last week, was a particularly busy one (in fact they are all busy), and there was one day where I felt quite weary, and consequently a bit low emotionally. You know those days when you just want someone to hug you two seconds longer than normal, or to say a kind word, or to just give you the push to keep going? So that afternoon, after the school activities run had been done for the day, I see lying on my bed a little rose that has been picked from my garden. The poor thing was probably parched lying there on my bed and the stem was cut a little short, so it was not suitable for placing in a vase or jug. I knew immediately that it was one of my children and a smile came to my face ... I found out a few minutes later who it was, and it deeply touched my heart. Along with the rose, was a big hug and a whisper of "I love you Mum."

Kindness is so often overlooked and underrated, yet for me, it carries such greatness and beauty. We can so easily overlook thoughtfulness but when you consider someone else above your own life and needs, it adds something rich and beautiful.

"When we show we care it makes others stand a little taller, breathe a minute and feel that strength that comes from support that is given not because it has to be but because it wants to be." (Charlotte Gambill)

Kindness is a beautiful way of displaying God's love and goodness, from the simplest acts such as a smile, or a compliment to grand, life-changing gestures. Many times, we perceive kindness to be 'silly' or maybe we think it has to inconvenience ourselves or it has to cost us one way or another. That is not true … Don't overlook it, as it potentially can unlock something so profound in another person. Live your life pleasing unto God, decide and allow it to become part of who you are, it can only add to your beauty and joy!

Live your life pleasing unto God, decide and allow it to become part of who you are, it can only add to your beauty and joy!

88

THE COST OF CONSISTENCY

"Consistency is not very glamorous but gee it is effective"

I saw this quote on Instagram yesterday and it is so very true! I love it because it simply summarises how we apply ourselves in life – whether it is discipline in exercise, parenting, loving people, serving, marriage and any relationship. The sad truth in life today though, is so often that powerful word "CONSISTENCY" is SO lacking. It is like the typical story of the tortoise and the hare … we all want the fast results as our lives are consumed with the "instant," with the quick and least amount of effort, and so unfortunately the consistency is often equated with slow, boring, overrated or possibly even painful!

There are just too many options to even write about when I think of consistency, but I do know that it is a word that I would like to be 'part and parcel' of who I am, and how I conduct myself in everything big and small! Consistency is frequently spoken about in several forums, but how that word plays out in your life is hugely important – well, to me it is! I am attracted to consistency for a few reasons – for me, it shows stability, maturity, loyalty, strength and it reaps huge rewards and blessings, not just for me.

We all know what is good for us, yet so often we desire the result without the effort. Take for instance the simple task of climbing stairs. We have a double story home, and so I climb stairs multiple times a day. I know it is good for me, but gosh it is tiring! One thing I do know is that is keeps me fit and my legs moving, but it also teaches me the value of the climb, moving from one level to the next. The consistency of climbing is so NOT glamorous as often I am out of breath, and yes even sweating, but it is effective! There are days when I can leap up the stairs, two at a time, and other days I seem to drag myself up, ever so slowly. Anything in life that moves you forward can also throw you backwards. Stairs keep your momentum consistent! Don't wish away your days, wanting to be on a different level or different floor as it "looks" better and easier. God will always promote, bless, bring favour and so often for me that has happened on the climb of the staircase I have started on. The beautiful thing is that He can bring you new landings / pauses you weren't expecting, amazing opportunities at different levels, and often new relationships and friendships as you climb. These are all things you miss in an elevator / lift (the quick and instant), that only has one direction and often no view of anything greater than its own confined space which is mostly stuffy and claustrophobic! The elevator / lift only teaches me how to press a button, limiting my capacity. It decides my journey and limits who can get in with me at any floor without my approval.

Daily, as I climb my stairs, I hope to remember that my commitment to consistency, even with some pauses and maybe at times slow and definitely not glamorous, it is massively effective. Onwards and upwards ....!

89

THOSE MOMENTS

You know those moments of looking at special photos of your children when they were little.
This photo of my little girl in my arms peeking over my shoulder with her little dimpled hand holding on, made me I realize that I won't be able to hold her like this in my arms for too much longer. The time is coming, when she will grow and change, and one day will stand next to me, shoulder to shoulder as a young woman. Even though I may not physically hold her like this when she is big, I will forever hold her in my heart, because I am her mother.

When she scrapes her knee, she comes running to me for love and "wound" dressing. When she has a bad dream or wakes up cold in the night, she seeks my bed for warmth and comfort. When her friends are mean and nasty, she tells me with big tears in her eyes that she feels sad and all alone. When she eventually lands on her feet after doing a cartwheel, she looks at me with total joy and satisfaction that she has finally "done it!" When she swims the full length of the pool, holding her breath, she opens her eyes and with damp eyelashes, her eyes light up with pride. These moments may seem silly, but for me they have become etched in my heart and mind as treasured moments.

I want to capture, treasure and remember these moments. I will remind myself to breathe in the smell of her hair, to hold that little dimpled hand, to feel her heartbeat against mine as I hold her in my arms, because all too soon, it will be just a moment that was cherished but never forgotten.

90

WHAT MY DADDY SAYS

Recently, I saw this beautiful clip on a child giving all these "facts" about nature and various other things. The interviewer asks him (when he could get a gap) how come he knows all of this and is it true? The young child (who is probably about 6) looks at him for a second and says, "Of course ... It is what my Daddy says!" I just love that he believes 100% that what his Dad has said or told him, is complete truth. There is no doubt, no wavering, no uncertainty, no second-guessing. This challenged me deeply as I thought, do I think like that about what MY father in heaven says about me, what He says to me and do I believe??

The bible mentions to have faith like a child ... it is pure, beautiful, untainted, uncomplicated, uncluttered. Too bad and how sad that we grow up and become full of nonsense. Do you remember at school (pre-school probably) where one kid would say "My Dad is the strongest because …. " and the next kid would answer and say, "No, my Dad way more stronger because he did this etc. etc." – eventually it would get so out of hand that these poor Dads had strength and powers like no other! But the truth is, our Dad is like that … He is mighty, He is strong, He is the alpha and omega, He is majestic, He is the truth, He is the way and He is the life.

I want to believe that what He says is truth! I mostly do, then I overthink it. Faith like a child doesn't overthink, he just believes, he just knows. So many of us believe other stuff, like what our society, friends, family or culture have said, and this can so often be the thing that makes us live so far beneath the promises that the Father has declared over us.

This is what He says …

- I am forgiven
- I am sanctified
- I am more than a conqueror
- I am free
- I am accepted
- I am created for good works
- I am a shining light

- I can do all things through Christ
- I am not condemned
- I am the righteousness of God through Christ Jesus
- I am an heir of God

To believe like that little boy about what his Daddy says, is absolute truth. This week and always, I want to believe it, live it and never let that truth go, that what my Daddy says about me and to me, is certain!

91

PIGGY IN THE MIDDLE

A few days ago, I was watching my younger children playing "piggy in the middle" – you know the game where the person in the middle has to try to catch the ball that is thrown between two others. This game has been around for absolute ages and is one of those "classic" kid outdoor games. The trick to getting the ball (if you are the "piggy" in the middle) is to outsmart the other two players and to anticipate their moves and jump and move a lot to get the ball. At one stage, I felt so sorry for my daughter who was just not able to get the ball in time, and so seemed to be stuck there in the middle for quite some time. In absolute frustration, she came crying to me that it wasn't fair, and the other two were being mean and not sharing. I had to tell her gently, although firmly, that the whole point of the game is to not let her get the ball, and in this case to NOT share the ball. She has to fight for it and put herself in their way in order to change the game plan.

Wow – what a lesson it was to me! I thought how true this was of how we view life and our situations … we so often have this "victim" mentality of how it is not fair (we all know the answer to that one, as we have been told this many times by our parents "life isn't fair!"), how we are always stuck and never get a chance …. you know that whine? Come on, we have all been there, done that, worn the t-shirt, taken-off the t-shirt and just as quickly put it back on, again and again!

To be stuck in the middle is sometimes the hardest place to find joy and contentment. This constant reminder of where we are NOT, and how we keep missing the ball or almost catching it, only to slip and drop it, is a very real frustration! It is exhausting both physically and mentally, and the option of giving up is so tempting. Let's face it, life isn't fair, and to outsmart the "balls" thrown at us, is quite something. Although, I had to remind my daughter that it doesn't matter how many times she misses that ball, it is about sticking at it, because it just takes one moment when she gets that ball and the game turns, and all those "dropped and missed balls" don't count anymore. As much as I was speaking to her, I felt God speak to me ... (I love how He does that!) I need to learn that being "stuck in the middle" is not forever, it can be frustrating and one feels like giving up, but it just takes that one quick moment, when I reach that little bit higher and catch the ball. The "stickability" of seeing a task through, is a wonderful life skill to teach our children and ourselves. Sadly, the culture of "giving up" because life is hard and unfair is so often the norm.

I have used the "piggy in the middle" game often to help her see things differently. The perspective one has when you are playing the game gives beautiful insight into how we respond to where we are at! Yes, in the middle of raising kids, life can be frustrating, it can be overwhelming, it is exhausting, it is trying to outsmart, outwit and outplay the opponents, but when that ball lands in your hands, it is exhilarating, wonderful and deeply satisfying.

Don't despise the season of "being the piggy in the middle" ... find the moment to enjoy the game, as you won't be stuck there forever!

92

UPPING THE GAME

I am not sure if you as a parent have felt that overwhelming (I think like breathing through one nostril while treading water) sense of having to "up your game" and make some real changes for some behaviour and other small things like attitudes, study schedules, manners etc. to be revisited and reformed? Well, for me, this week was one of THOSE weeks!

It never ceases to amaze me that these gorgeous little humans who we get to raise, default so often to their "sin" nature. The odd huff when asked to do a chore, the casual roll of the eyes or the back-chat! Jeepers, there is ZERO tolerance for this in our home – like zip, nil, naught and again did I mention ZERO tolerance. Sadly, what can happen so often is that one can ignore this as just being "teenagers" or "they are going through a phase" but actually, let's be honest here ... that is a rebellion monster that grows so quickly with little feeding!

So, this week, firstly I had not been feeling so well or in top form (not sure what top form is but I guess it is anything where one doesn't feel exhausted?) We had had a full weekend of activities and so when the week started on Monday, it felt like we left the starting block with a bit of a limp. I won't bore you with the day to day challenges we have had with one or a few kids simultaneously, but I will tell you that we (as husband and wife) had a moment in the kitchen, when we locked eyes with a fierceness of a challenge, and without uttering words we both decided in that moment of a few seconds that we had to "up our game" in some areas that were looking rather messy! It is in those moments, that I am so massively grateful to God that we are a united front, a team that is unshakeable on certain core values and so together we can gently and firmly guide and correct our children.

So often when we feel least likely to challenge and correct, and our "guard" is down, that is when we as parents need to "up our game" – by "game" I mean, spend more time in prayer, have more intentional conversations with our children by putting away distractions (i.e. devices) and look them in the eyes and have those "tete-a-tete" talks (lovely French phrase meaning head to head – you ain't get closer than head to head talks) YES, it is not fun, lovely and rosy ... but it is necessary, it is SO worth it and it brings clarity when life is blurry and hazy!

93

THE NO FUN PARENT

There have been times (maybe a few too many in the last little while) where I feel like I am the "no-fun" parent. I have moments where all I feel like I am saying is "NO" ... "no you can't have pudding every night" Why they ask "Well, firstly we don't have puddings every night because it is not good for us and they are considered treats." Then "Don't pour the shampoo in the bath to make bubbles" Why they ask, "Because shampoo is for hair and it is too expensive to waste in the bath" But it's like having soap in the bath which just takes away the dirt without the effort of washing ourselves. "Good point, I think to myself, but again re-iterate that possibly it's not the best move and let us rather keep shampoo for what it is intended" And so it goes on and on ... see what I mean – the "no-fun" parent. Sometimes I irritate myself!

Why – I even ask myself that question. Maybe I should just say sure eat pudding every night, pour the shampoo in the bath and lather up kiddos ... I mean, what really is the big deal. It's not dangerous and certainly not life threatening, yet I find myself in this state of being the person who kind of kills the joy with the rules. I sometimes wish I could be THAT person who let's their kids eat marshmallows and ice cream for supper and lets them paint one another with fabric paint because after all it is being creative, FUN and allowing them some freedom. It really isn't such a big deal, is it? But you see for me, I see the end ... I see the fall out that will come after the sugar rush has crashed, the crying from sore tummies and then possibly holes in teeth that need filling, and then the paint that although says it is fabric paint is not and accidentally, gets smeared on Dad's car or the walls!

The truth is that in this little phrase of being the "no-fun parent" there is an important word there that I take very seriously, and that is parent. I want to do this well and so that means that sometimes (and quite often) I have to BE the parent and by that, I mean, set the borders and parameters. Yes, I also must relax somewhat and choose the battles with wisdom, and not always be the kill joy! The wonderful thing about parenting is that we start off in small doses ... setting the small boundaries before the spaces get wider and bigger. We start off with the training of eating and sleeping, manners, tidying-up, being kind, sharing etc. and then it gets to bigger arenas ... God is so gracious to us but sadly so often we try bypass those boundaries and leap ahead only to be cool, fun, hip and happening and our kids' mates. You are not supposed to be your kids' friend (until they are older) – you are supposed to be their parent (definition: bring up, look after, take care of, rear, hand-raise) and sometimes that means being a little less fun ... for now!

94

BE STILL

It has been a while since I have written, and mainly because my life has been full (like everyone else's too). I also decided when I first started to blog over 2 years ago, that I would not just fill a page with words just for the sake of writing, but rather I wanted it to be a little more meaningful than a random rambling. So there has been lots going on in our lives, but today I decided to sit quietly after doing some admin and ponder and ask God what He wants to show me and teach me. The house is silent ... bliss, and it is just me at home today.

The crazy thing is, that as mothers we tend to feel guilty when we are "still" and quiet because we may think it is being lazy or passive or something negative. I have been pondering over this beautiful scripture in Psalm 46: 10 "*Be still and know that I am God!*" – I love the translation in The Message where is says – "Step out of the traffic! Take a long, loving look at me, your High God, above politics, above everything!"

So often, we equate "being still" with doing nothing! All of us immediately disqualify ourselves, because when do we ever as mothers or women ever really do 'nothing?'

The word still is a translation of the Hebrew word rapa, meaning "to slacken, let down, or cease." In some instances, the word carries the idea of "to drop, be weak, or faint." It really is best described when two people are fighting until someone separates them and makes them drop their weapons. It is only after the fighting has stopped that the warriors can acknowledge their trust in God. We often interpret the command to "be still" as "to be quiet in God's presence." While quietness is certainly helpful, the phrase means to stop frantic activity (HELLO mothers!), to let down (Yes, let that hair down, chill a little), and to be still. For God's people being "still" would involve looking to the Lord for their help.

You see, being still and doing nothing are two different things. While I am "still/ceasing my frantic activities", I am not doing nothing, as I am choosing to trust my God. To trust is a doing word, a verb which means I am doing something! The word translated "trust" in the Bible literally mean "a bold, confident, sure security or action based on that security." Trust is not the same as faith, which is the gift of God (Ephesians 2:8-9). Rather, trusting is what we do because of the faith we have been given.

As the year starts to get a little more intense and frantic with ballet concerts, school exams, projects, Christmas activities, prize-giving etc. etc., I need to … "step out of the traffic "and take a long look at my God who is higher than all these things!

Take the gaps, make the change and shift the focus from frantic (panicky) to calm (being still)!

95

PRESSING PAUSE

Don't you sometimes wish you could press pause on your life, in the middle of the chaos and 101 demands? Imagine being able to press pause, so that firstly you could breathe – deeply, then perhaps drink a hot cup of tea and finish it to the last drop, and then maybe finish a conversation with a friend or perhaps a spouse without anyone or anything interrupting (not even a waitron), or maybe until you could catch up on some payments before the next one looms around the corner AGAIN! Sadly, time is inevitable and waits for no man, nor woman, nor child!

I am reminded how every year, especially at this time of year when life does seem to escalate in terms of demands, there is often that weary look in our eyes, that overwhelmed look of "my eyes are open, but no one is home!" (Yes, I thought so ... I am not imagining it at all.) We can all identify and although we may all be at different levels and intensities, we are all in fact trying to make it to the end of the year without too many limps, fractures or breaks along the way.

In my brief years of mothering, I have learnt and am still learning that there are times when we oversee the remote of our lives. We can pick it up (yes, we do own it and it won't bite) and press pause! For some reason (some strange reason) so often many of us are too scared to do that … WHY?! No one else can press pause of our own movie, our own life, only we can. To press pause and create boundaries and protect our little family (ok I know it is not little, but you know what I mean) to take some time away from the hurly burly, is vital to our sanity and strength.

These are some of the the "pause" moments we have created and maybe you can identify with them too:

1. We allow our children two days a week where they just go to school and do nothing *extra* afterwards as this becomes their "afternoon off" (besides obviously doing homework and their school requirements.) So many parents complain of their hectic lives, yet they signed

their kids up for extra-murals (key word here is *extra*). So, this means that you are the responsible person who has involved them, and so they are doing *extra* things that fill their day and yours.

2. We are intentional about eating together as a family at the table every night. Yes, there are those evenings when things do go a little crazy and we end up eating in staggered sittings, but for the most part, we sit together as a unit and chat. It is amazing how much we hear at the supper table about school, friends, life etc. It is a beautiful "pause" moment.

3. As parents, we take some pause moments too, as our kids know that after 8pm, it is our exclusive "Mum and Dad" time and they (the older ones as the little kids are already fast asleep) need to go to bed to read and sleep soon after.

4. We plan for family holiday times (usually only once a year that this happens) and try in creating memories. It is a "pause moment" of being together, investing into each of our lives in an environment away from home.

5. We celebrate victories and have those "pause" moments especially when it comes to birthdays. It is not about a huge party or elaborate, expensive gifts, but rather it is a time when we honour the birthday person, celebrate their life, their dreams and cheer them on into their bright future.

I understand just like everyone, life is full, and it is not as simple as it used to be, BUT we can order our own world and make moments count. I encourage you as you are "treading" the waters of life being crazy as the year hurtles to an end, to take pause moments … because you can!

96

IT WASN'T ME

I don't know if anyone else has this phrase go around in their household, but in mine it is very common and used multiple times in one day.

For example, …
Mum asks – "Who made tea and left a mess?"
To which the response is …. "It wasn't me!" even
though all 5 happen to be drinking tea at that precise
time!!!! REALLY ….!?!

I have often thought why do they always deny it and shift the blame? Why don't they just accept it, own it and deal with it, but I guess their response reflects their lack of maturity to own it, accept it and deal with it. Or maybe, if they deny it, it will go away, and they won't get blamed. Yet, I guess as 'mature' adults, we have the same attitudes in most situations. We deny the bad attitude, the offence, the harsh words, and often pretend we are justified firstly, and secondly that if we don't admit it, it will go away. Well, the truth is it doesn't! All it does is follow us around and it becomes baggage that only weighs us down and makes us "heavy and uncomfortable"!

Nothing much else has changed really since the beginning of time when Eve blamed Adam and Adam blamed Eve for partaking in the 'forbidden fruit' ... the typical *"blame, name and shame game!"* You see when God asked the profound question in Genesis 3 – "Where are you Adam?" (which of course HE already knew as HE is God and all knowing) He wasn't asking the obvious, but rather He wanted Adam and Eve to own up and admit what they did. This was not for his punishment to be unleashed on them, but rather for Him to forgive them and rescue them from their sin. Instead Adam chose to hide from God. Their sin had destroyed his fellowship with the Lord. God knew this, and He was pointing it out to Adam. Man is on the run before God because he knows that he is guilty before God. However, God comes and seeks us and wants to re-establish a relationship of mutual love. It is God who takes all necessary steps to make this possible again. That is the story of the Bible, the story of love that is always pursuing us, from the first to the last book "Now the dwelling of God is with men, and he will live with them. They will be his people and God himself will be with them and be their God." (Revelation 21:3)

I am trying my best to show my children that mistakes are inevitable, but denial is not Godly. They know many of my vulnerabilities, and I am weak and faulty in so many areas, but I will always try to display to them that no matter what, I can own my own issues, 'stuff' and mess and say sorry, and it is ok!

97

CLEAR ROOM MAKE SPACE

For anyone who knows me well, I often change my furniture around in our home and regularly declutter, tidy-out and re-sort. As you can imagine, this is something that happens often in our home and with 5 children, it is so necessary as all to quickly "stuff" overtakes us. There is something so therapeutic about chucking out and organizing … well for me it totally is. I am not one of those people who can turn a blind eye to chaos and mess, and so this is a very essential part of how I manage our home.

I have had these words in my head and heart for months now and have been waiting and wanting to "flesh" this out more. I feel this is what God has been saying to me personally, as well as for my family and in every area of my life …

Clear room make space ….

The recent conversations I have had with close friends has been very much around this thing of how we manage and simplify our lives and lifestyle, replenish our souls and find rest. Every second person I hear is asking this same question of why are we so busy, why are we so tired and overwhelmed?

Just like in a room where there is too much furniture or things, all too often, we put our own stuff in our lives and then wonder why we bump into it, injure ourselves or shuffle around it. We allow our lives to become cluttered all too quickly with MORE than – whether that is too much stuff materially, or too many commitments, or too many activities. For me, when I have cleared my wardrobe or eliminated extra stuff in my home that is not needed or used regularly, it almost allows me to breathe easier and it calms me. The simplicity of the clearing room, making space physically, also allows me to see clearer and feel more at peace. Yet, I feel that this is more than a physical thing. In my soul and spirit, I need to get back to basics. What are those basics you may ask?

For me this is a few of my own basics:

- Pray – often and always – in the car, while cooking, over our children … in every moment of the day – big moments or small.
- My default setting is and will always be the WORD OF GOD before opinion of man. Read the Word. That's it – just do it!
- Make space for a few minutes a day of peace and quiet time of learning to LISTEN. No distractions, no social media, phones, devices etc. Just listening … it can just be in the car on the way to collect children from activities – no music, no radio … give it a try.
- Intentional conversations of looking into the eyes of the person speaking and fully being present – not thinking of a zillion things like what to make for supper etc.

There is a reason why part of the armour of God is shoes of peace. We need to walk in them every day – it may seem obvious, but it is a daily decision and commitment to follow HIM.

Maybe life is all too much and overwhelming (I know what that is like) and yet I choose to clear room, make space for what He is and wants for me, as His daughter.

98

THE RACE

This year has already been quite a mile-stone year in a few ways and one of the things I wanted to experience and be a part of, was the epic Two Oceans Marathon in Cape Town. So, with that goal in mind, the training started, and it was hard! As running doesn't come naturally to me, it was a sacrifice but becoming fit was also the goal, so it began, and I must admit that I did enjoy that process even though at times I felt I was not improving at all.

The day arrived, and I felt as ready as I could be, but was still quite nervous as I was doing this race alone (i.e. no running partner or friend) yet not lonely as there were another 15 999 other runners! We all waited in the dark at 4am until our time start at 6.20am. It was freezing cold due to an icy wind, yet the atmosphere was alive and buzzing. One of the incredible attractions of running, is the camaraderie of people with the common goal of running to finish. Many of us stood together huddled against the wind with our black plastic bags over our kit to help keep the chill away. I met such friendly chatty people most of whom were from Johannesburg (we do have VERY friendly people.) As we lined up in our thousands, the announcer played the national anthem and it was incredibly moving as all races, genders, creeds stood together united and this loud chorus filled the darkness, then we were off ...

The support of locals along the way, and the jostle of runners for the first 5km was amazing (I had kind of been dreading the start as to find a "running rhythm" can be a dodgy start), but it was so much fun and still more conversations were had. The scenery as dawn broke was just exquisite and much laughter and joking was heard as we all ran our way through suburbs and climbed some hard hills etc. (that is where the chattiness became less and less as we all tried to just breathe.) Every competitor wore their race numbers on front and back along with one's name printed in bold black letters. One of the most stand out moments were when people who you never met, nor would possibly ever meet again, screamed along the side lines ... "Go Jennifer, you can do it!" That's what we need to be doing with one another in this race called life – encouraging and applauding!

My family were waiting for me along the way, and to see their happy faces and enthusiasm was so rewarding, and it gave me the push to finish strong. As I heard and saw the finish line, the passion and cheering gave me the last boost to run faster and harder to get to the end. It was an amazing feeling crossing that time mat, and for me it was a massive achievement. I know for those who run long regular marathons, a half marathon is your average training day … and for that I salute you! For me, however, it was just as huge as I never EVER thought I could or would run as far as I did. I was asked would I do it again? The answer is YES – for sure!

99

WHEN I CAN'T FIX IT

Our year started off with some real challenges. Without going into too much detail, our son Connor was very ill and spent two and a half weeks in ICU and thereafter in the neurological ward in hospital due to a severe brain abscess. I know you are asking right now "How on earth does one get an abscess on the brain?" - Good question! It is very rare and yet here we were facing some very serious decisions. One being surgery (which of course had huge risks) and the alternative was the slow steady treatment of IV meds, which could also not quite penetrate the infection and consequently he could have ended up in surgery anyway.

It was a very hard, exhausting time as one of us had to be with him constantly as he was so sick and in so much pain. The pain was hardly controllable until the swelling came down which again was subject to the antibiotics penetrating the infection which had been "sealed-off" by the brain in order to protect it from exploding (gross I know … but that is the truth) In between nausea, fevers, vomiting, drips, IV's, swabs, blood tests, CT scans, MRI scans and countless specialists consulting, he was discharged and sent home to recover. He missed the first six weeks of school and is still not allowed to do any physical activity for the next six months. The treatment, although slow was the most beneficial as it allowed the body with the meds to slowly nail this infection and we are still treating him with good probiotics etc. in order to establish strength and the "good stuff" back into his body. We were in very good hands with excellent Neurosurgeons, Neurologists and ENT specialists but more than that we had the GREAT PHYSICIAN totally part of this whole process and leading and guiding us together with the doctors.

I will be honest, there were times I felt so overwhelmed! Never-mind the sheer exhaustion of the total lack of sleep in ICU and hospital wards, there was the constant watch as to what the nurses were doing, and not doing in between the doctors' rounds (that is a WHOLE another story!) There were also many situations and decisions we had to make on behalf of our son. Many times, we had to stand together as husband and wife, mother and father and ask God our Father to show us what to do, every little decision and every big decision. Of course, emotions are fully charged, and everyone is fragile due to the severity of the diagnosis, yet there was this constant reassuring peace that rested on us, each one of us. There were times when I had to dig very deep and trust Him when I felt so completely shattered and numb and could not see how this would turn out. To see your child in constant pain, and I cannot fix it, was incredibly hard.

The beautiful gift in this all was the constant prayer we felt through our dearly loved family and friends, near and far. The practical visits from popping in with coffee (sometimes as early as 6am, friends would arrive at hospital to give us a hug and a coffee), sometimes it was the random conversations of other patients and their families which created a slight distraction, and then to meals at night for the rest of the gang at home was so incredibly helpful and a huge blessing. The odd night, my Dad stayed in hospital with Connor in order to give us a break and I know that that time was hugely significant for my son as his grandfather, his "Papa" spoke life into him, and told him stories (many stories) of his childhood, experiences with God and about deep stuff and silly stuff. Connor to this day, still talks and laughs about Papa's stories and the songs and music they listened too while passing time with drips running, meds being changed and all that stuff that happens in the long days and nights in hospital.

For the most part, I was strong and felt the grace of God over carry us but there were a few moments when I cried - a lot! I sometimes would sit in the corner of the hospital room, stifling the sobs that would rise as I did not want my son to hear or see how I struggled with seeing him so sick. I would have swopped with him in a heartbeat for him to be pain free and well, as I am sure every mother or parent would do. Other times, I would be strong and then a friend would pop in and look at me a little longer and be a little more tender, and I would lose the plot and want to do the ugly cry. I realized in those moments of being so fragile and real, that it wasn't a weakness (as we so often believe) but rather a pressure valve of releasing the tension, the pent-up emotions and the sheer relief of allowing myself to be human!

Through it all though, and now on the "other side" of the sickness, we are stronger, more dependent on God as our Rock and Anchor and know that no matter what we face, we can trust Him with this. So often we want to work it all out. I don't know why he got sick or why it got to the terrible state it did, but I do know that in everything, God was with us.

- Through the fights with medical insurance, He gave us strength and strategy and people who could offer advice and stand with us.
- Through the confusion as to why some meds made him sicker, there was common sense thinking that enabled the doctors to think through things differently and adjust things.
- Through the sleepless nights and disturbed interruptions of changing drips etc., there was a peace and a grace that was supernatural.
- Through the absent parenting to our other children, friends and family stepped in and help carry the load. There was a grace too as despite our lives being very disruptive, they were secure and happy.
- Through the tireless questions and chatting with nurses and staff, we were able to share Jesus to them.
- Through the quiet moments of waiting, our strength was renewed.

- Through the moments of exasperation and desperation of willing him well, the strength of prayer carried us, and courage was upon us and I know that I know that it was only because of God - there is no other explanation.
- Through the dark days and moments when we felt low and so discouraged, family and friends were praying and standing in those gaps for us and were obedient to give us encouraging words and dreams and hopes.

Despite the moments (and there were many moments) of feeling low, exhausted and overwhelmed, I know that God my Father was with me, with Connor and our family. I never felt forsaken nor forgotten.

I couldn't fix it, nor take it away, but I could keep walking. So, step by step, moment by moment, I did just that and chose to celebrate the victories and to not be too discouraged by the challenges or supposed set-backs. I could take my son's hands and put them with full confidence in the hands of his loving Heavenly Father, and in the multiple times when I couldn't answer his questions, I told him that God knows and to ask him. Sometimes being the parent and admitting that I am weak, faulty and imperfect allows me to show off just how good and perfect Jesus is!

We were never asked to fix it, but to rather fix our eyes on Jesus, the perfecter of our faith!

ABOUT THE AUTHOR

This book is written to encourage mothers in the journey of raising Godly children. The 5 Gems reflects her heart in not only parenting, but character, life, marriage and virtues.